Drupal 8 SEO

Content Highlights:

Drupal 8 SEO Checklist

Working faster with Coffee

Redirects

URLs and paths with Pathauto

Metatags

XML Sitemap

Google Analytics

Schema.org with RDF

Better internal linking

Validating HTML and CSS

Fixing broken incoming links

Page-by-page keyword optimization

Figuring out which optimizations worked with Diff

Secure and speedy sites

Ranking with Accelerated Mobile Pages (AMP)

Social link building with AddToAny

My goal with this book is to show marketers how to achieve SEO results with Drupal 8 with a minimal need for developer help. From checklists that help you work faster to Metatags, XML sitemaps, and beyond—this book is exactly how I would execute on-page SEO for a client. If you're trying to achieve high rankings and get more leads and sales from a Drupal website, then this book is for you.

––Ben Finklea

Drupal 8 SEO

The Visual, Step-by-Step Guide to Drupal Search Engine Optimization

Ben Finklea

www.Volacci.com

13359 Hwy 183 N, Suite 406-270, Austin, Texas 78750

Drupal 8 SEO

Copyright © 2017 by Volacci Corporation

FIRST PRINTING: January, 2017

International Standard Book Number: 978-1-946017-00-0

Printed in the United States of America

Trademarks

All terms mentioned in this book that are known to be trademarks or service marks have been appropriately capitalized. Volacci Corporation cannot attest to the accuracy of this information. Use of a term in this book should not be regarded as affecting the validity of any trademark or service mark.

Warning and Disclaimer

This book is designed to provide information about Drupal 8 and SEO. Every effort has been made to make this book as complete and as accurate as possible, but no warranty or fitness is implied.

The information is provided on an as-is basis. The author and Volacci Corporation shall have neither liability nor responsibility to any person or entity with respect to any loss or damages arising from the information contained in this book or from the use of the programs or add-ons that may accompany it or are recommended by it.

Cover design by popdesign☼

Table of Contents

About the Author

Ben Finklea has been working on the Internet since 1995. He has started four companies, and he is currently the CEO of Volacci. He lives near Austin, Texas which is every bit as cool as you've heard.

A graduate of Texas A&M University, Ben is a frequent speaker at conferences on the subjects of Digital Marketing, Drupal, and building successful high-tech businesses. He is the author of Drupal 6 Search Engine Optimization (Packt, 2009) and created the Drupal *SEO Checklist* module (https://www.drupal.org/project/seo_checklist) which has been downloaded over 300,000 times by Drupal site owners worldwide.

Ben has built and managed SEO campaigns for many companies including HP, Fast Company, Oracle, State Farm, Acquia, and Amazon.

Ben is married to Dr. Beverly Finklea. Their sons, Andrew & John, are active in Boy Scouts and Brazilian Jiu-Jitsu. As a family, they sing in the choir at Emmanuel Presbyterian Church in Cedar Park, Texas.

LinkedIn: https://www.linkedin.com/in/benfinklea

Twitter: https://twitter.com/benfinklea

I am continually updating the content in this book as the Drupal and SEO worlds change and grow. For weekly Drupal SEO updates, information, errata, and news, please sign up for the **Volacci Drupal Marketing Brief Newsletter** here:

Volacci.com/newsletter

This book is dedicated to the memory
of my father-in-law, Robert Wendon "Bob" Reed.

Thank you for being there.

About the Reviewers

Tracy Cooper

Tracy is a Jack of All Trades with experience in technical writing, web development, customer success management, and digital marketing. She is currently a Drupal marketing specialist at Volacci. In her spare time, Tracy is an avid gamer and hosts an online radio show. She lives in Austin, Texas.

Mike Taylor

Mike is the owner of Weaving Media Design, based in the Philadelphia area. He works with clients ranging from small non-profits to large manufacturing concerns. His passion is education and he has been involved in online education for over 20 years. His latest endeavor is Weaving Knowledge which serves the needs of hybrid training for business.

Mike O'Connor

Mike O'Connor has spent the last decade immersed in Drupal and eCommerce. He was a core contributor to both Drupal 6 and 7, as well as maintaining and contributing to numerous Drupal modules, including Drupal Commerce. Mike currently works as an eCommerce consultant. In his spare time, he enjoys running an organic farm in Michigan with his wife and kids.

Foreword

Marketing departments are choosing Drupal more than ever before. With Drupal 8, marketers can create engaging designs with Twig, tie Drupal's data layer into new digital interfaces like Amazon Alexa, or integrate Drupal with third-party marketing tools and analytics systems. Plus, the editorial experience is better than ever. Our new WYSIWYG editor makes it easy to author content and the in-place content editing means faster website updates without IT support. However, marketers must answer one question before they choose Drupal: How well will my website rank in Google?

The short answer is very, very well. In fact, Drupal's ability to rank well in Google is a competitive advantage to the companies that use it. From the NBC Olympics to Tesla Motors; from NASCAR to the NFL Super Bowl; from the White House to our own Drupal.org, Drupal does extremely well in search rankings.

Drupal sites rank highly in Google because Drupal is developed by thousands of contributors. As new SEO requirements come to light, the Drupal community builds modules to address them. Updates are contributed in hours or days while other platforms wait weeks or months to catch up. This model of rapid community innovation creates a real advantage to marketing-driven organizations that choose to adopt Drupal.

But how does one evaluate the thousands of modules that exist? Which modules will solve today's SEO problem best for your use case? Which modules have been adopted into Drupal 8 core and which ones will no longer be maintained? How should these modules be used and configured?

You are holding the answers in your hands. This book makes Drupal-specific SEO approachable. It does an excellent job of explaining how to SEO your website: which modules to use and the exact steps needed to install, configure, and implement them.

It's exciting for Drupal, too. The more Drupal 8 sites are search-engine optimized the right way, the better marketers will feel about Drupal overall. As Drupal's reputation as an excellent marketing platform grows, Drupal grows.

I'm pleased that Ben is sharing his hard-won knowledge of SEO with us and I look forward to using these techniques on my own websites.

Dries Buytaert

Founder and Project Lead, Drupal (Drupal.org)
Founder and CTO, Acquia (Acquia.com)
Young Global Leader, World Economic Forum (Weforum.org)

Acknowledgements

I would like to thank the following people for helping me create this book:

My wife, Beverly, and my sons, Andrew and John. You are why I do what I do. I love you so, so much!

The Drupal community for making amazing software. You are an open-source beacon of hope in a closed-source world.

All the Drupal core contributors and module maintainers who build the tools that I use every day. I tried my best to name you all throughout the book—apologies if I missed anyone.

Travis Carden who co-maintains the SEO Checklist module with me.

Jeff Geerling (geerlingguy) the creator of DrupalVM which I used extensively in creating this book.

Karen McNeill and Donelda Cox from The Spectrum Services Group who helped with the editing and inspired ideas for the book.

Jay Hilscher who listened to me vent my frustrations when I hit roadblocks.

The D.O.N.s 2—Nancy Stango, Eric Mandel, Andrew McClenaghan, Andy Kucharski, and Mohan Sunkara—for advice and moral support.

Finally, to God who extends me grace and forgiveness every day.

Introduction

"The base paths belonged to me, the runner. The rules gave me the right. I always went into a bag full speed, feet first. I had sharp spikes on my shoes. If the baseman stood where he had no business to be and got hurt, that was his fault."

Ty Cobb
BASEBALL PLAYER

TY COBB HAD A REPUTATION (untrue, as it turns out) for sharpening the spikes on his shoes to razor sharpness. He felt like the base paths belonged to him and if a fielder got in his way, well, that was the fielder's fault.

I'm not advocating playing dirty with your SEO. I do believe in competing hard to reap the greatest reward from the search engines. Like Cobb, we should do everything we can within the rules to win.

As many readers are undoubtedly aware, I've spent a good deal of time and energy on the subject of Drupal SEO over the last ten years. I have spoken at countless Drupal conferences, developed SEO training, and wrote Drupal 6 Search Engine Optimization (Packt, 2009) all while running Volacci—a Drupal SEO company. You might say that I eat, drink, and sleep Drupal SEO.

As is always the case, technology moves quickly on. Both Drupal and SEO have changed enough in the last seven years that I felt that it was time for a new book. And that's what you're holding in your hands right now.

If Any Three of These Are True, You Need This Book

Not sure if *Drupal 8 SEO* is for you? Let's make it easy. If at least 3 of these are true, then this book is for you:

1. **You've got a Drupal 8 website**. Either you took it over, your company built it, or you're about to launch a new endeavor and Drupal 8 is the right technology you need to get the job done.

2. **You need a Drupal 8 SEO shortcut.** This book is the shortcut to getting your Drupal 8 site optimized, ranking, and working for your business.

3. **You already use the Drupal 8 SEO Checklist module.** I created this book to be a supplement to the SEO Checklist module for Drupal 8. If you're already using the module, this book is for you.

4. **You've invested a lot in Drupal 8 already.** All the hard work your team has done to create a great website will go to waste if you don't generate a steady flow of customers ready to buy, sign up, or join.

5. **You're not looking for an SEO education.** This book is short on SEO "whys" and long on Drupal 8 "how-tos." Instead of rehashing common SEO concepts, I've linked to trusted online resources that explain the basics.

6. **You've SEO'd another platform and need to SEO Drupal.** Drupal does SEO differently. This book will empower you to be more productive and fruitful using Drupal best practices (also known as The Drupal Way).

7. **You can implement a solid SEO strategy yourself.** This book will help you put that strategy into practice.

8. **You need to rank in the search engines.** Ranking well in Google matters. A lot. It's not an afterthought—or at least it shouldn't be—but, rather, it's at the forefront of your mind as a marketer.

9. **Winning matters to you.** Companies that rank well in Google win. Companies that don't rank are not even in the running—it's just that simple.

10. **You're a visual person.** They say a picture is worth a thousand words so there are over 150 annotated Drupal 8 screenshots in this book. My goal is for you to see precisely what to do, where to click, and how things work.

The Drupal SEO Checklist Module + Book

For a while, I kept a long note taped to my Mac listing the SEO modules that I used on every Drupal site. That sticky note became the *Drupal SEO Checklist* module. It eliminates guesswork by creating a functional to-do list of tasks. You can find out more and download it here: https://drupal.org/project/seo_checklist.

While the *SEO Checklist* module gives you a long list of *what to do*, it doesn't do anything to explain *how to do it*. That's where this book comes in. **I designed *Drupal 8 SEO* to follow the *SEO Checklist* module describing how to implement SEO for Drupal 8.**

This Book Gets Straight to the Point

If you were sitting at the desk next to me right now and you needed help with an SEO problem, I'd just tell you how to solve it. I'd even walk you through the steps so you could move on as soon as possible. That's what this book is. It's me telling you how to solve your Drupal 8 SEO troubles as quickly as possible.

I left out the long, basic SEO explanations. There are many great resources online with full explanations of how SEO works, what Google's looking for, and how to win the online marketing game. I'll link to some good ones so you can dig deeper when you need to. I love Moz.com, especially their Beginners Guide to SEO— https://moz.com/beginners-guide-to-seo.

Don't feel that you're missing out on great SEO knowledge! **I left in the best parts: the exact SEO and Drupal 8 how-tos.** The fewest SEO steps that you need to get the job done on your own with as little help as possible from your Drupal developer. (If you're a developer, no offense—I love you folks, but you're so darn busy that it's hard to get things done at times.)

Will it work? It should work pretty well. You're a great marketer. I'm the Drupal SEO guy. We should be able to get it done together, right? Just in case that's just not enough, here's my email address: ben+drupal8seo@volacci.com. Email me. (The '+drupal8seo' alerts me when your email arrives so I can get back to you expeditiously.)

What You Can Expect from This Book

This book explains the way I would do SEO on a Drupal 8 website. It's not the only way, but it's the best way. After search engine optimizing hundreds of Drupal sites over ten years, I've learned which methods work best, the quickest shortcuts, and the order in which to do things.

The widest possible compatibility, the stability of the website, and the long term SEO outcome are the keys to success because let's face it, you don't want to do this again. I use the straightforward methods, not the sexy new way of doing things. ("Headless Drupal" can be a disaster for SEO if implemented improperly.)

One final point is that I do this for a living. If you get through this book—or just get too busy—and your site is still not ranking as it should, then get professional help (https://volacci.com/contact). It's worth it. Feel free to contact me and I'd be happy to help or point you in the right direction.

How to Read This Book

I recommend you do everything in Chapters 1 and 2 to give you a good foundation for understanding and executing on the rest of the book. Chapters 3-10 were written to follow the SEO checklist from top to bottom. You can either go straight through or just skip to the sections needed when you need them.

Use the *SEO Checklist* module. Check things off (and click save) as you complete them. It will help you keep track, and it makes a great report to give to your client or boss when your SEO tasks are finished.

So, thanks for buying this book! I hope that it inspires you to do even more with Drupal 8.

Conventions Used

Annotations

Throughout the book, you'll find various text styles to help make concepts clearer or to draw your attention to important aspects of a task. Here are some examples:

- *Italics* — warnings or critical terms
- **Bold** — new words or to draw attention
- Code — URLs or code snippets
- "Quotes" — interface elements you're interacting with

> **Notes, Tips, Warnings**
> **Extra information that might help you better understand a concept, avoid a misstep, or give you additional functionality.**

> **SEO Training Camp**
> **Outside reading that will help you understand an SEO topic.**

SEO Checklist tasks are marked with "□"

I created this book and the Drupal 8 SEO Checklist at the same time. They're made to go together. As such, I've designated a checklist item with a square like this one: □. That way, when you've completed that item, you know to check it off on the SEO Checklist in the admin section of your site.

Difficulty Level

Throughout the book you'll notice icons like these:

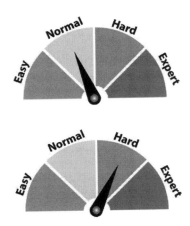

Sometimes, it can be helpful to know how hard a task is going to be, so I've included them to make things clear. Here's what they mean:

- **Easy**: Straightforward and quick.
- **Normal**: A bit more involved, maybe 2 or 3 separate steps but no heavy lifting.
- **Hard**: It's going to take some thought and time to do this. Still, most marketers should be able to knock it out with some effort.
- **Expert**: This task is time-consuming, technical, or difficult. You may need to get some help from a Drupal developer to get it done.

SEO Training Camp

SEO Training camp is outside reading that will get you up to speed on various topics. They're SEO concepts covered in more detail than in the book. Read them if you're interested, but they're optional.

Chapter 1: Getting Started with Drupal 8 SEO

"If you're not first, you're last!"

Ricky Bobby

TALLADEGA NIGHTS:

THE BALLAD OF RICKY BOBBY

Items Covered

- Key Drupal Concepts
- Warning about *alpha*, *beta,* and *dev* modules
- Three ways to install a module
- A list of SEO modules for Drupal 8
- Browser tips

CONGRATULATIONS ON BUYING THIS BOOK—the first ever published with the step-by-step, technical details you need to search engine optimize a Drupal 8 website. It is the first step to digital marketing excellence that will reward you with increased ranking, traffic, customers, and sales.

Drupal 8 SEO

Drupal 8 is the content management system of choice for sophisticated enterprise websites because it was built from square one with the anticipation and extensibility needed to optimize every node, every view, and every snippet of code for search engines. That is, of course, if you know how to configure it.

Search Engine Optimization (SEO) has been around for many years and you likely understand the basic concepts. Drupal 8 has only been out since November of 2015, so there is plenty yet to learn about this fantastic new content management system.

With many new additions to ease-of-use, functionality, and robustness, Drupal 8 is the superior method for creating and marketing your website to the world. For all its improvements, Drupal 8 still feels like Drupal—faster, cleaner, more refined, and more up-to-date, but still Drupal, nonetheless.

One thing that didn't change, though: *Drupal is phenomenal for SEO*. I've worked in Drupal for ten years and experienced firsthand how positively search engines respond to a properly-optimized Drupal site. Customers have tripled traffic in weeks after upgrading from another platform. Drupal has competitive advantages from site-wide optimizations like RDF or AMP that put my clients on the cutting edge of SEO. The benefits are higher rankings quicker and more traffic.

Unlike previous versions, Drupal 8 has scheduled feature releases at six-month intervals. We won't be waiting around for years if a new technology like responsive design, HTML 5, or CSS 3 comes along.

Despite these continuous releases, the admin interface is relatively stable so the screenshots in this book should be accurate.

Key Drupal Concepts

Let's discuss a few key concepts that you need to know about if you're new to the Drupal community. (Long-time Drupalers can skip this part.)

The Drupal Community

Drupal is more than just software. It's a community of people. Who makes up that community? It's made up of the people who use Drupal. That's you! Congratulations, you are now part of the Drupal community. Welcome!

The community is a club (scores of local meetups), it's a group of companies (Acquia is just the biggest of many businesses in the Drupal community), and it's an organization (the Drupal Association). But you can be involved without ever touching any of those entities.

Many people first get involved in Drupal by downloading the software and then, when help is needed or confusion arises, asking for assistance on Drupal.org. That's a common way of getting to know the community. The more involved you become, the better time you'll have using the software. It's nice to use tools made by people you know.

Drupal Core and Drupal Contrib

Throughout this book, I refer to **Core** and **Contrib**. It's important to understand the difference, so you know where to go for help if something isn't working right.

All Drupal sites run a version of the Core Drupal project—**Core** for short. The extra contributed modules, contributed themes, and custom code that are installed are what make each project unique. Together, these contributed modules and themes are referred to as **Contrib**.

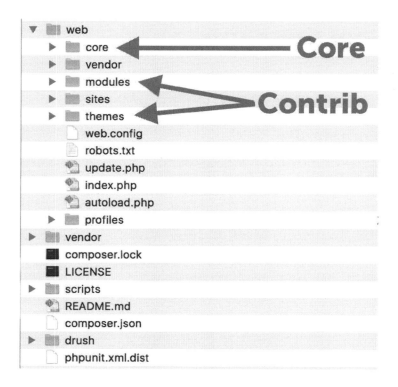

On your server, Core is in the `/core` directory. Everything else is Contrib or custom—you'll see a /libraries, /modules, /themes, /vendor, and a few other directories.

To make it as simple as possible:

- *Core* features are built-in to Drupal.
- *Contrib* features are added-on to Drupal.

The Drupal community has created tens of thousands of Contrib modules. Every once in a while, a widely-used and well-written Contrib module is added to Core. This is one of the ways that Drupal Core gets new features. In fact, with the release of Drupal 8, several modules and functions that used to be Contrib are now included in Core. This means less installation, less code for you to update, and a more stable website.

A Warning About Contrib

The Drupal community develops contrib modules and themes. That means that anybody with a problem to solve (or ax to grind) can build a module and publish it on Drupal.org. Be careful when you decide to install community-contributed code on your Drupal site.

Near the bottom of the project page for a module, you'll see something like this:

Version	Download	Date
8.x–1.0–beta10	tar.gz (64.04 KB) | zip (163.78 KB)	2016–Aug–22
7.x–1.17	tar.gz (196.4 KB) | zip (279.44 KB)	2016–Jun–30
Development releases		
Version	Download	Date
8.x–1.x–dev	tar.gz (65.18 KB) | zip (168.67 KB)	2016–Sep–16
7.x–1.x–dev	tar.gz (204.82 KB) | zip (295.38 KB)	2016–Sep–19

This example comes from the *Metatag* module:
https://www.drupal.org/project/metatag.

Notice that there are different versions of the module. The 7.x or 8.x on the left tells you the compatibility with the major versions of Drupal. The -1 or 1.0 tells you what major version of the module. Finally, the –beta9 or .17 tells you the minor version of the module. A green highlight means that it's the version of the module that is recommended by the maintainer.

So, 8.x-1.0-beta9 means that this module is compatible with Drupal 8, it's the 1.0 version of the module, and it's in beta 9 which is a prerelease version. Since it's highlighted in green, it's the recommended version.

> *Warning: Install new modules on a development server and test them thoroughly before you push them to live.*

Installing a Drupal Contrib Module

The page at https://www.drupal.org/documentation/install/modules-themes/modules-8 has good explanations of the primary ways to install a module. If you're working with a developer, ask her the best method as it can vary based on your server configuration, security, access levels, and what's already installed. Below are the most popular methods.

Installing a module using the Drupal admin interface

This method is the easiest but least-secure way to install a Drupal module. It's not secure because you're required to enter your File Transfer Protocol (FTP) password which is then transmitted in an unencrypted way to your server. If your enterprise security alarm bells are going off, skip this method. However, if you are practicing "security by obscurity", this method is quick.

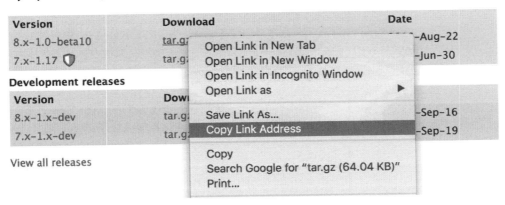

1. Copy the URL of the module file from the module's project page on https://drupal.org/.

2. Go to the Extend page: Click **Manage > Extend** (Coffee: "extend") or visit http://yourDrupal8site.dev/admin/modules in your browser.

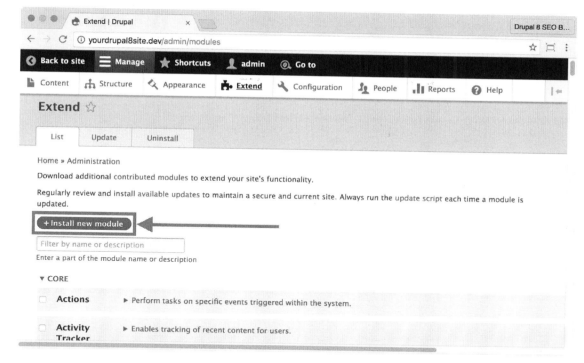

3. Click the **+ Install new module** button and follow the prompts.

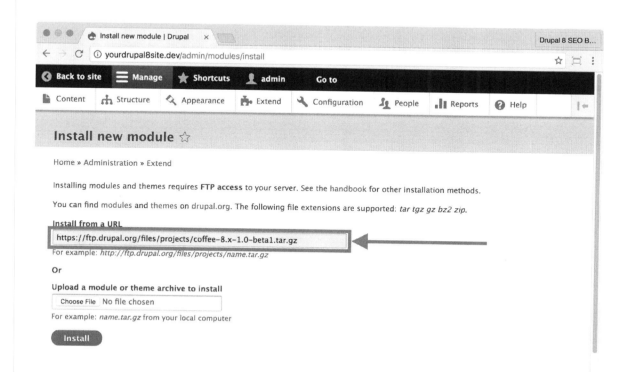

4. Paste the URL from step 1 into the **Install from a URL field**.

5. Click the **Install** button.

You will see a confirmation screen like this one:

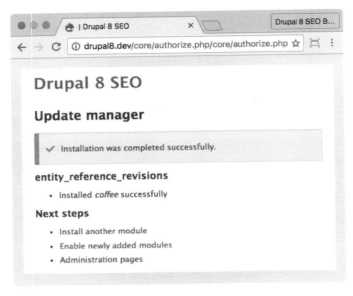

Installing a module using SFTP

If your server supports SFTP, then you can securely upload modules to the server.

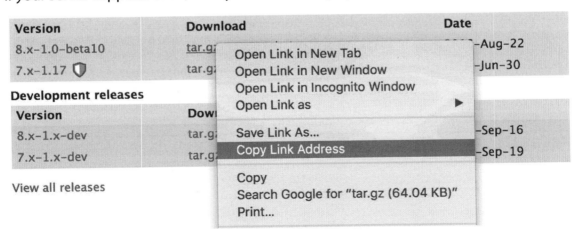

1. Download the module from the module's project page on https://drupal.org/.

2. Extract the files. The downloaded module package will be in a compressed file such as 'tar.gz'. Extract it using your system's extraction program. Often, you can double-click the file and Windows or macOS will extract it for you.

3. Using an FTP program like *WinFTP* on Windows or *Transmit* on macOS, login to your server.

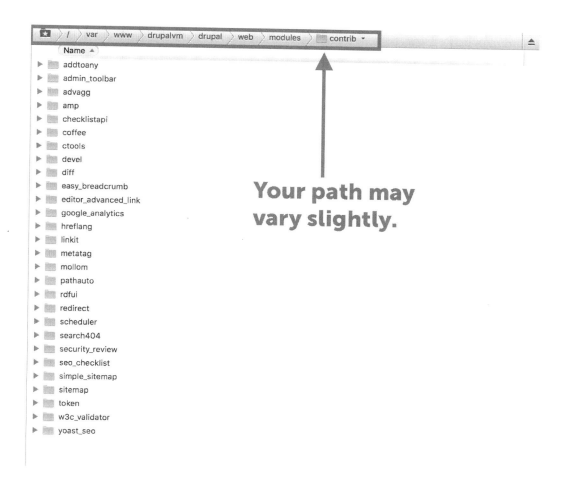

4. Upload the extracted Contrib module folder to the drupal/web/modules/contrib folder on your server.

Installing a module using the command line: Composer, Drush and Drupal Console

Using command line tools like Composer (the PHP package manager), Drush (the DRUpal SHell), and Drupal Console (the new Command Line Interface for Drupal) can be the fastest and easiest way to install modules for the more technically-savvy marketer.

These Command Line Interfaces (CLI) are powerful ways to manage your Drupal 8 site, update Core and Contrib, and more. Most marketers aren't going to get this deep into the technical side of things, but if you're a techie marketer (like me), these tools can save you hours every day.

1. SSH into your Drupal server. (If you don't understand this step then you should skip this section.)

2. Navigate to your Drupal installation.

3. Enter the command for the system that you're using:

   - Composer: composer require drupal/*module_name*
   - Drush: drupal module:download *module_name*
   - Drupal Console: drupal module:install *module_name* –latest

---

SEO Training Camp
- **https://getcomposer.org/doc/00-intro.md**
- **https://drupalconsole.com/docs**
- **http://docs.drush.org/en/master/**

List of Contrib Modules to Install

Here are the modules that you will install as you SEO your website while going through this book. It may be easier to upload them all at once—just don't enable them yet.

> *Note: There is a difference between "installing" a module and "enabling" a module. Installed modules are on your server, but Drupal does not run the code. Enabling the module means that Drupal is now executing that code, bringing the functionality into your website.*

SEO Checklist module - https://www.drupal.org/project/seo_checklist

Admin Toolbar module - https://www.drupal.org/project/admin_toolbar

Coffee module - https://www.drupal.org/project/coffee

Pathauto module - https://www.drupal.org/project/pathauto

Redirect module - https://www.drupal.org/project/redirect

Metatag module - https://www.drupal.org/project/metatag

XML Sitemap module - https://www.drupal.org/project/xmlsitemap

Alternate hreflang module - https://www.drupal.org/project/hreflang

Google Analytics module - https://www.drupal.org/project/google_analytics

Easy Breadcrumbs module - https://www.drupal.org/project/easy_breadcrumb

RDF UI module - https://www.drupal.org/project/rdfui

Linkit module - https://www.drupal.org/project/linkit

D8 Editor Advanced link - https://www.drupal.org/project/editor_advanced_link

W3C Validator module - https://www.drupal.org/project/w3c_validator

Sitemap module - https://www.drupal.org/project/sitemap

Search 404 module - https://www.drupal.org/project/search404

Yoast SEO module - https://www.drupal.org/project/yoast_seo

Diff module - https://www.drupal.org/project/diff

Scheduler module - https://www.drupal.org/project/scheduler

Mollom module - https://www.drupal.org/project/mollom

Advanced CSS/JS Aggregation module - https://www.drupal.org/project/advagg

*AMP module - https://www.drupal.org/project/amp

*AMP theme - https://www.drupal.org/project/amptheme

*AMP PHP library - https://github.com/Lullabot/amp-library

Share Buttons by AddToAny module - https://www.drupal.org/project/addtoany

Prerequisite modules required by some of the above:

Checklist API module - https://www.drupal.org/project/checklistapi

Ctools module - https://www.drupal.org/project/ctools

Token module - https://www.drupal.org/project/token

*the AMP suite requires you to use Composer to install.

Permissions

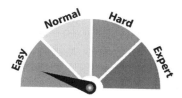

You need permission in Drupal to use the modules called for in this book. Drupal is quite secure, and one of the ways it remains secure is with a robust, multi-layered permissions system. If you're working with a developer, you'll need to ask them to assign a role to you that has the "Administer permissions" permission.

Here's a helpful email that you can send to your developer:

Dear *Jill*,

My username on the yourDrupal8site.dev web server is *<your username here>*. Please grant my account the "Administer permissions" permission.

http://yourDrupal8site.dev/admin/people/permissions#module-user

I will be working with some new modules for SEO and I need to give myself permissions as I go.

<OPTIONAL> It may be a good idea to create a "Marketing User" role for this, but I'm open to your suggestions on the best way to grant me the access I need.

Thanks!

<your name>

Awesome Marketer

Helpful Browser Tips

How to View Source of a Webpage

Sometimes, I'll instruct you to "view source". It's easy: in your browser, there is a command to view source. Here's how to find it:

Chrome: View > Developer > View Source

Firefox: Tools > Web Developer > Page Source

Edge: … menu > Developer Settings > Check 'Show "View source'…". Save and the option will be there in the Context menu.

How to use an Incognito Window

An incognito window is like a new browser. It doesn't have any of the cache, cookies, login data, browsing history, etc. It's a fast and easy way to see what a new visitor to your website will experience.

Chrome: File > New Incognito Window

Firefox: 3 bar menu > New Private Window

Edge: … menu > New InPrivate window

Conclusion

We've covered the basics, and now you know a lot more about Drupal SEO from a 50,000-foot perspective.

- I've warned you about installing dev, alpha, and beta modules on your site (make a backup of everything and use a dev server!!!)
- You know how to **install a module**, if you need to.
- You know what modules you're going to be working with over the next nine chapters.
- You **requested permissions** to use the modules.

In the next chapter, we're going to make sure you are as fast and efficient as you can be by installing the **SEO Checklist** module, **Coffee** module, and **Admin Toolbar** module.

> **Warning: Final notice: BACKUP YOUR DRUPAL SITE. Make sure you (or your developer) knows how to restore it if something should go wrong.**

Chapter 2: Be Efficient

"But first, you gotta get speed. Demon speed. Speed's what we need. We need greasy fast speed!"

Mickey "Mick" Goldmill
ROCKY II

Items Covered

- Module Filter
- SEO Checklist module
- Coffee module
- Admin Toolbar module

GETTING GOOD AT DRUPAL and SEO is a lot more fun if it's easy and fast to find the settings pages that you need when you need them. Installing and setting up just a few helper modules can make a big difference in the enjoyment and efficiency of this process.

This chapter is about the helper modules that make me more efficient. I install them on most Drupal 8 sites that I work on.

Module Filter

One of the handiest modules that moved from Contrib into Drupal 8 Core is the *Module Filter* module. This module adds a filter to the Extend section of Drupal admin. It allows you to quickly find the Core and Contrib modules installed on your site.

When you go to **Manage > Extend**, you'll see a field that says "Enter a part of the module name or description" under it.

This easily-missed field saves a lot of time when installing (and uninstalling) modules. If you've recently installed a module but haven't turned it on yet, use the module filter to narrow your choices and find the new module. Begin typing the name of the module into the field and Drupal will display any modules that match.

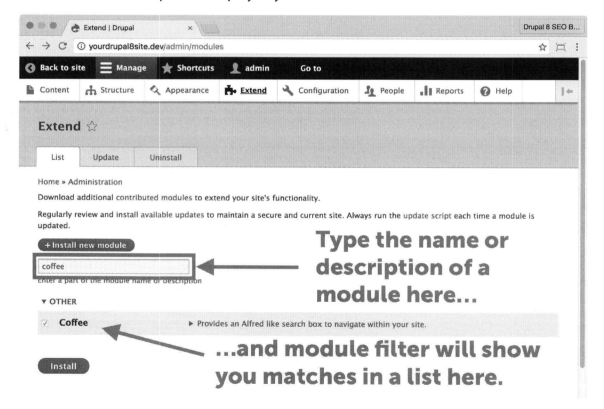

To enable a module, select the checkbox next to it and click the blue **Install** button. Drupal installs the module and you get the functionality that the module provides.

Drupal SEO Checklist Module

https://www.drupal.org/project/seo_checklist

The *Checklist API* module is required:

https://www.drupal.org/project/checklistapi

Credits & Thanks

Thank you to Travis Carden (TravisCarden on Drupal.org) for helping me create and maintain the SEO Checklist module. Travis also created the required *Checklist API* module.

About the SEO Checklist Module

The Drupal *SEO Checklist* module uses Drupal SEO best practices to check your website for proper search engine optimization.

The *SEO Checklist* module and this book were designed to work together. While the *SEO Checklist* module tells you what to do, this book tells you how to do it. Over the course of this book, we'll be going through the *SEO checklist* module one task at a time, explaining in more detail how to do each task and sometimes even a bit of why each item is needed.

As a module, the *SEO Checklist* does several helpful things that will speed up your work and learning curve.

- It provides a to-do list with checkboxes of the SEO steps needed to optimize your Drupal 8 site. There are modules to install and tasks to complete, organized by function. Since you own this book, you've got the one-two punch for Drupal SEO.

- It checks for installed modules and, if it finds them, checks them off for you.
- It adds a timestamp and username to track task completion.

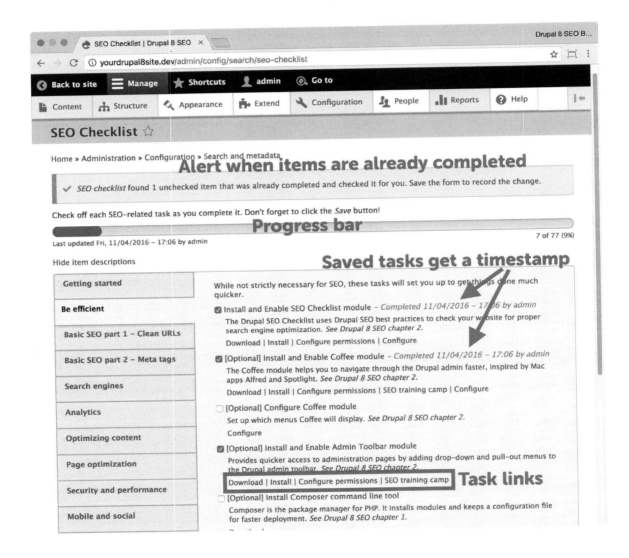

> **Tip: Remember to click the Save button each time you check off an SEO Checklist to-do item or if an item is checked off for you!**

☐ *Install and Enable the SEO Checklist Module*

1. Install the *SEO Checklist* module on your server. (See Chapter 1 for more instructions on installing modules.)

2. Go to the Extend page: Click **Manage > Extend** (Coffee: "extend") or visit `http://yourDrupal8site.dev/admin/modules`.

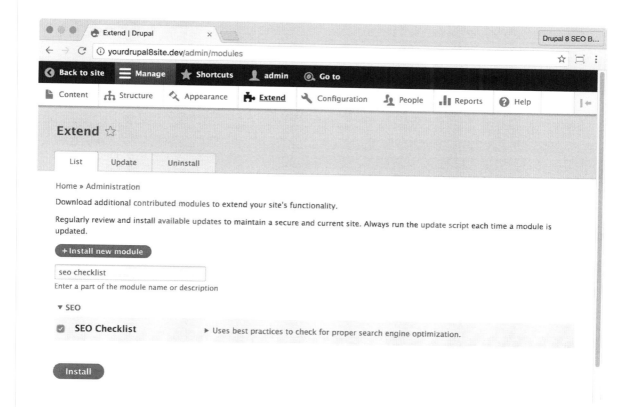

3. Enter "seo checklist" into the module filter field to quickly find the *SEO Checklist* module.

4. Select the checkbox next to "SEO Checklist" and click the **Install** button at the bottom of the page.

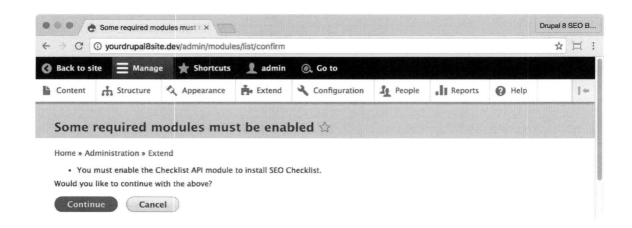

5. You may get a message stating, "You must enable the Checklist API module to install SEO Checklist. Would you like to continue with the above?" If so, click the **Continue** button.

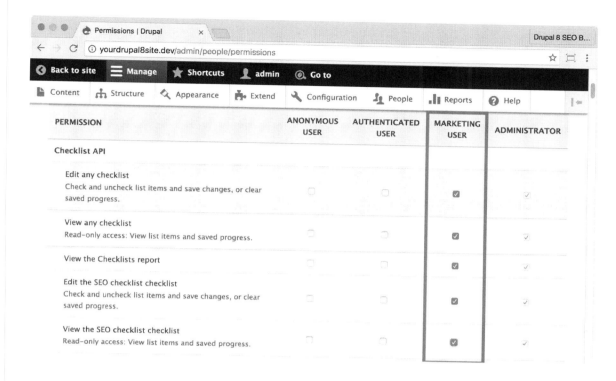

If necessary, give yourself permissions to use the *SEO Checklist* module.

1. Click **Manage > People > Permissions** (Coffee: "perm") or visit http://yourDrupal8site.dev/admin/people/permissions.

2. Select the appropriate checkboxes for

   - "Edit any checklist"
   - "View any checklist"
   - "View the Checklists report"
   - "Edit the SEO checklist"
   - "View the SEO checklist checklist" (Yes, the word checklist appears twice.)

3. Click the **Save permissions** button at the bottom of the page.

Using the SEO Checklist module

To use the SEO Checklist module:

1. Go to **Manage > Configuration > Search and metadata > SEO Checklist** (Coffee: "seo") or visit
`http://yourDrupal8site.dev/admin/config/search/seo-checklist`
in your browser.

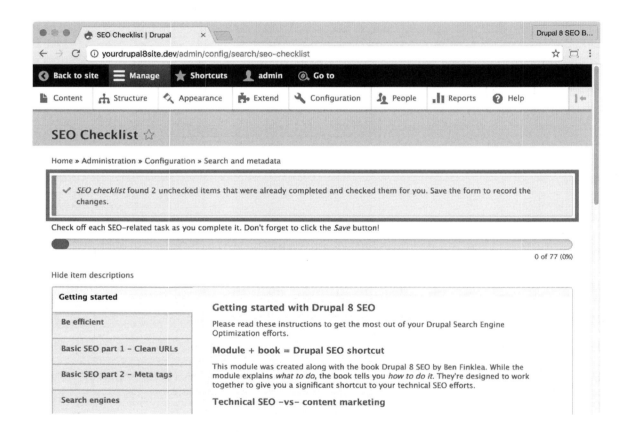

2. You may see the message, "SEO checklist found *X* unchecked items…". If you do, it means that there are some tasks already completed. Nice! You're ahead of the game. If this happens, click the **Save** button near the bottom of the page.

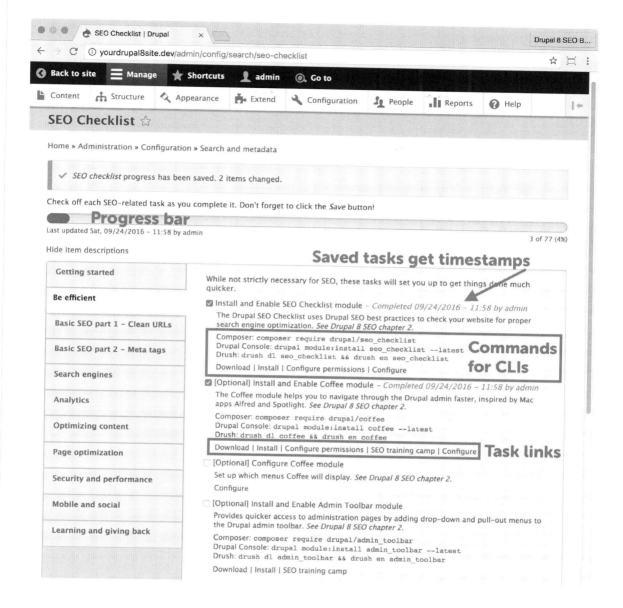

3. Click on the **Be efficient** tab. You'll notice:

- A progress bar that shows you how many tasks remain;

- Timestamps on your saved tasks (if you've done any yet);

- Commands for Composer, Drupal Console, and Drush;

- Task links to help you quickly get things done.

You'll also notice that the tabs on the SEO Checklist follow the chapters in this book. You can easily follow along and check things off as you go.

To make the SEO Checklist even easier to use, be sure to turn on chapter numbers or page numbers. Doing so will add a corresponding page number to each item. When you're ready to do that item, flip to that page in this book for more info and a how-to guide.

As you continue on your Drupal 8 SEO journey you can use the SEO Checklist module to make sure you've done all you can to get the most out of your Drupal 8 site.

> *Tip: Many steps throughout this book start with going to an admin page, permissions page, etc. The links on the SEO Checklist are another, even quicker way to get there.*

The Coffee Module

https://www.drupal.org/project/coffee

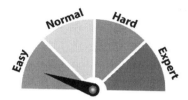

Credits & Thanks

Thank you to Michael Mol (michaelmol on Drupal.org) for creating and maintaining the *Coffee* module. Thank you to Marco (willzyx), maartenverbaarschot, and Alli Price (heylookalive) for your contributions.

> *SEO Training Camp*
> **https://dev.acquia.com/blog/drupal-8-module-of-the-week/drupal-8-module-of-the-week-coffee/12/04/2016/10291**

About the Coffee Module

The *Coffee* module is the fastest way to get to any admin screen in Drupal. As you SEO your Drupal 8 site, you will spend a lot of time jumping into admin to change a setting or check on updates. You'll have to go through menu navigation if you don't have the *Coffee* module. That's fine, but sometimes it's hard to remember where every single setting is.

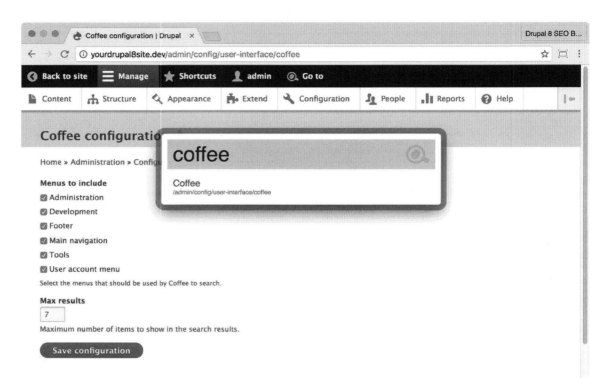

With the *Coffee* module installed, you can type ALT-D on your keyboard (Option-D for macOS) to have a text field pop up. Start typing into this field and the *Coffee* module will show you the admin menu items that match. Press the **Enter** key to select the first item or use the arrow keys to select a different item and press the **Enter** key to go directly to the admin page that you want.

> *Tip: Throughout this book, I'll give you* **Coffee** *shortcuts when appropriate. If I say Coffee: "extend", then you'll hit your Coffee shortcut keystroke (Alt-D or Option-D) and type "extend". Now, you're Drupaling like a pro!*

☐ *Install and Enable the Coffee Module*

1. Install the *Coffee* module on your server. (See Chapter 1 for more instructions on installing modules.)

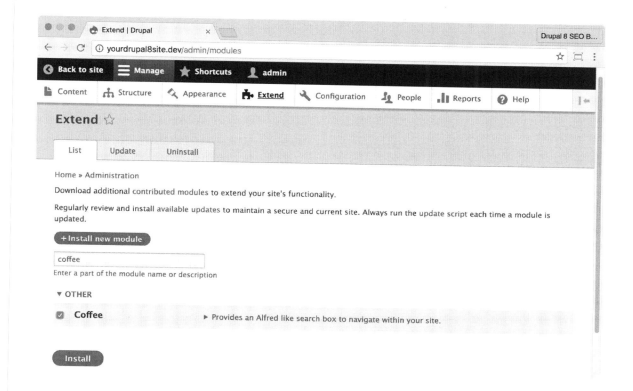

2. Go to the Extend page: Click **Manage > Extend** (Coffee: "extend") or visit `http://yourDrupal8site.dev/admin/modules`.

3. Select the checkbox next to "Coffee" and click the **Install** button at the bottom of the page.

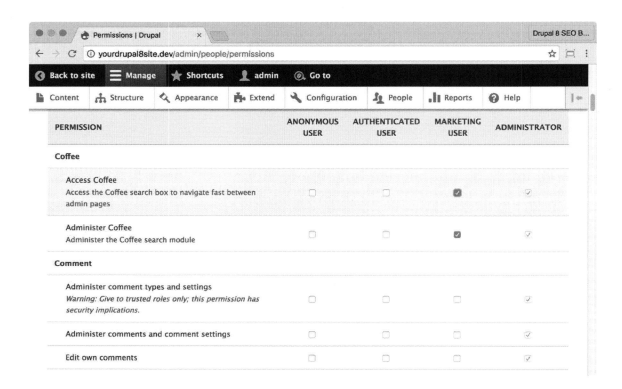

If necessary, give yourself permissions to use the Coffee module.

1. Click **Manage > People > Permissions** (Coffee: "perm") or visit
   `http://yourDrupal8site.dev/admin/people/permissions`.

2. Select the appropriate checkboxes for

   - "Access Coffee"
   - "Administer Coffee"

3. Click the **Save permissions** button at the bottom of the page.

☐ *Configure the Coffee module*

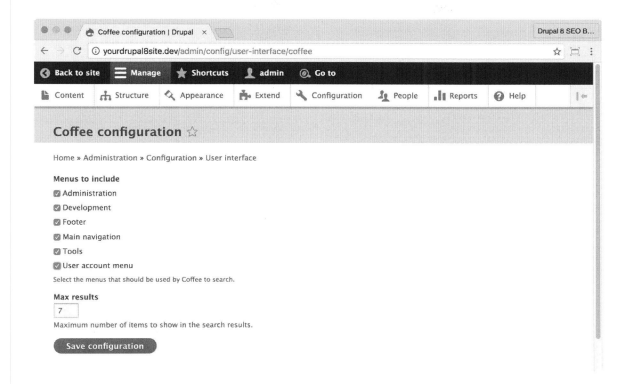

1. Go to the *Coffee* admin page: Click **Manage > Configuration > User Interface > Coffee** (Coffee: "coffee") or visit `http://yourDrupal8site.dev/admin/config/user-interface/coffee`.

2. Select the checkbox next to any additional menus that you want to include in the *Coffee* interface. I typically include them all, but if it starts getting cluttered, then you can take them out later.

3. Click the **Save configuration** button at the bottom of the page.

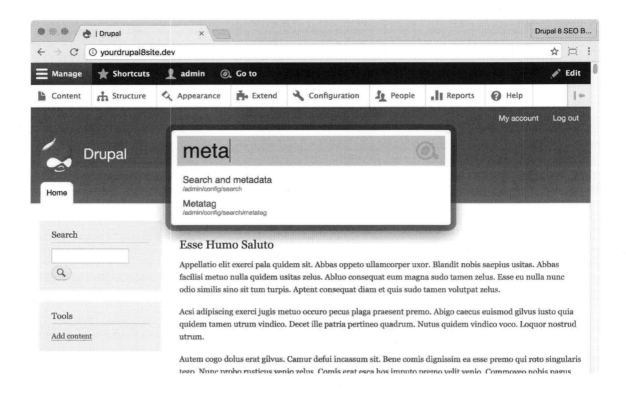

The *Coffee* module makes getting to the right admin screen much quicker.

The Admin Toolbar Module

https://www.drupal.org/project/admin_toolbar

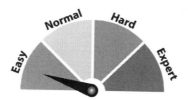

Credits & Thanks

Thank you to **Mohamed Anis Taktak** (matio89 on Drupal.org) for creating and maintaining the *Admin Toolbar* module. Thank you to **Romain Jarraud** (romainj), and **Wilfrid Roze** (eme) for their contributions to this module.

> *SEO Training Camp*
> *https://dev.acquia.com/blog/drupal-8-module-of-the-week/drupal-8-module-of-the-week-admin-toolbar/04/02/2016/9661*

About the Admin Toolbar Module

The *Admin Toolbar* module gives you one-click access to Drupal 8 admin screens. It works like the drop-down and slide-out menu system that is so popular on the web.

While I prefer the speed and ease-of-use of the *Coffee* module, there are times I need to see the hierarchy. The *Admin Toolbar* module provides that ability.

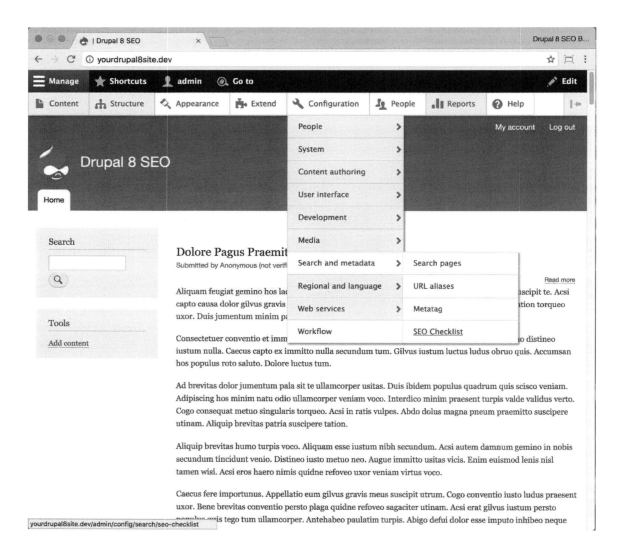

☐ *Install and Enable the Admin Toolbar Module*

1. Install the *Admin Toolbar* module on your server. (See Chapter 1 for more instructions on installing modules.)

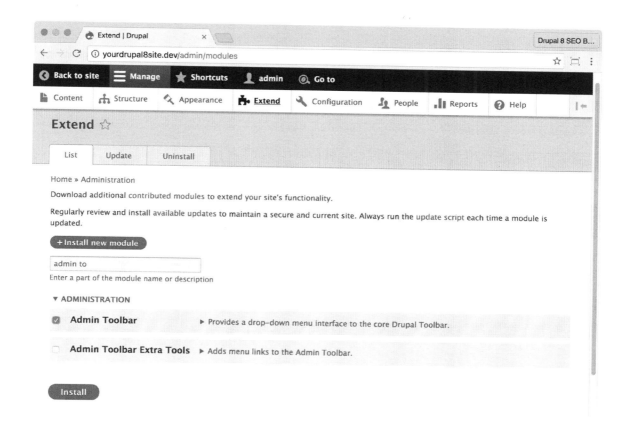

2. Go to the Extend page: Click **Manage > Extend** (Coffee: "extend") or visit `http://yourDrupal8site.dev/admin/modules`.

3. Select the checkbox next to "Admin Toolbar".

4. Click the **Install** button at the bottom of the page.

The *Admin Toolbar* module uses the Admin menu permissions. If you can access the Admin menu, then you have the permissions you need.

Conclusion

We covered four SEO Checklist items in this chapter. You've added modules that are going to make the next steps in optimizing your website much easier.

- We kicked things off by explaining how the **module filter** works on the Extend screen.
- You installed the Drupal 8 ***SEO Checklist*** module and turned on chapter or page numbers.
- You installed the ***Coffee*** module—the fastest way to get around in Drupal admin screens.
- Finally, you installed the ***Admin Toolbar*** module making it easy to browse the admin section.

In the next chapter, we start on the SEO side of things, beginning with the basics: Clean URLs, setting up your site to automatically create paths, and redirects.

Chapter 3:
Basic SEO Part 1 — URLs

"Go pick me out a winner, Bobby."

Roy Hobbs
The Natural

Items Covered

- Clean URLs
- *Redirect* module
- *Pathauto* module
- *Pathauto* patterns

IN THE SIMPLICITY OF THAT famous line from The Natural, it is perhaps easy to forget the hours spent creating the unique bat that Bobby handed to Roy Hobbs. Earlier, the two worked together to select the lumber, cut out the shape, sand, and seal it.

URLs and paths lay the groundwork for many other aspects of SEO. They're the hardest thing to change once they're set, so it's important to get them right. They're powerful enough to turn a good site into a great one. In this chapter we're going to "pick out a winner" by optimizing your site's URLs, setting up redirects, and creating *Pathauto* patterns for keyword-rich paths.

☐ Enable Clean URLs

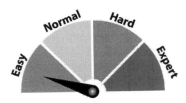

A query string is text in a URL preceded with a "?". Drupal's "clean URLs" rewrite query strings into human-readable text. Query strings get in the way of search engines. Google's not bad at understanding URLs with query strings, but it does not always get it right. Make sure your URLs don't contain query strings.

Clean URLs are installed on your Drupal 8 site by default and cannot be turned off. But, it is possible that the proper software isn't installed on your server, so it's worth checking, just to be sure.

> *SEO Training Camp*
> **Enable Clean URLs docs: *https://www.drupal.org/node/15365***

How to tell if clean URLs are enabled

1. Open an Incognito window (see chapter 1) and go to the homepage of your website.

2. Click on a piece of content on your site. You need to navigate to an actual blog post or node, not the home page.

3. Look for "?q=" in the URL.

A. If the URL looks like this: http://drupal8.dev/my-blog-post-title then clean URLs are enabled and you can skip to the next section of the book.

B. If the URL looks something like this: http://drupal8.dev/?q=node/4 then clean URLs are not enabled. Continue in this section.

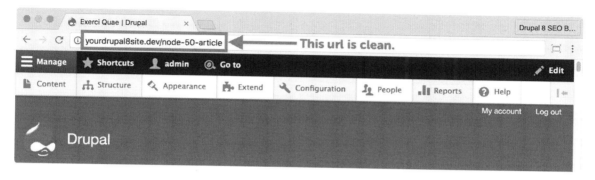

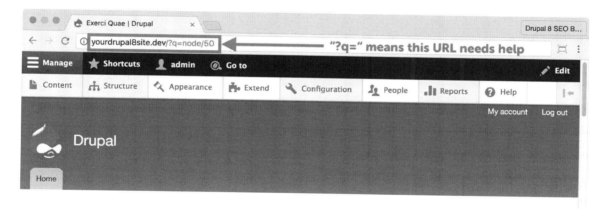

The URL on top is "clean". The URL on the bottom is "dirty".

How to fix your URLs if they are dirty

Here's the good news: there's nothing you can do yourself to fix your dirty URLs. You need to get in touch with your developer or hosting company and say this magic sentence:

"It looks like my URLs are dirty because I'm seeing "?q=" in the paths. Would you please enable mod_rewrite for Apache on my server?"

You can point them to this URL: https://www.drupal.org/getting-started/clean-urls#dedicated which explains things in more detail, but the magic sentence above will normally get the job done.

Once mod_rewrite is turned on, you should use an incognito window to test it again.

The Redirect Module

https://www.drupal.org/project/redirect

Credits & Thanks

Thank you to Moshe Weitzman (moshe weitzman on Drupal.org) for creating this module. Thank you to Dave Reid, Sascha Grossenbacher (Berdir), and Jonathan Hedstrom (jhedstrom) for your help maintaining it.

> *SEO Training Camp*
> *https://moz.com/learn/seo/redirection*

About the Redirect Module

The *Redirect* module redirects visitors from old URLs to new URLs. When you've moved a piece of content to another section of your site or inadvertently changed the URL, this module can really help.

> *Note: In previous versions of Drupal, you needed both the* **Redirect** *and* **Global Redirect** *modules. In Drupal 8, they are combined into the* **Redirect** *module, streamlining your SEO efforts.*

The *Redirect* module creates *301 redirects* from old URLs to new URLs on your website. 301 redirects help your SEO by making sure that any URL that ranks in Google will still resolve when a visitor arrives. If you don't install this module, you will have to regularly look for any URL that changed and fix them. There are reports in Google Search Console that can help, but it's better to prevent missing pages from the start.

This module highlights the power of Drupal, automating what used to be an arduous and ongoing SEO chore. Thanks to the power of Drupal 8 and the *Redirect* module, fixing links is a much less frequently needed task.

☐ *Install and Enable the Redirect Module*

1. Install the *Redirect* module on your server. (See Chapter 1 for more instructions on installing modules.)

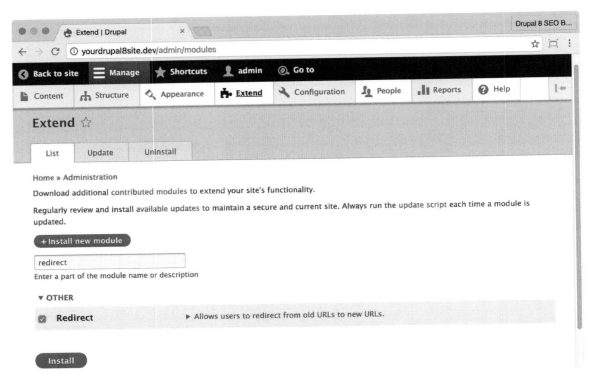

2. Go to the Extend page: Click **Manage > Extend** (Coffee: "extend") or visit `http://yourDrupal8site.dev/admin/modules`.

3. Select the checkbox next to "Redirect" and click the **Install** button at the bottom of the page.

If necessary, give yourself permissions to use the *Redirect* module.

1. Click **Manage > People > Permissions** (Coffee: "perm") or visit `http://yourDrupal8site.dev/admin/people/permissions`.

2. Select the appropriate checkbox for "Administer URL redirections".

3. Click the **Save permissions** button at the bottom of the page.

☐ *Configure the Redirect module*

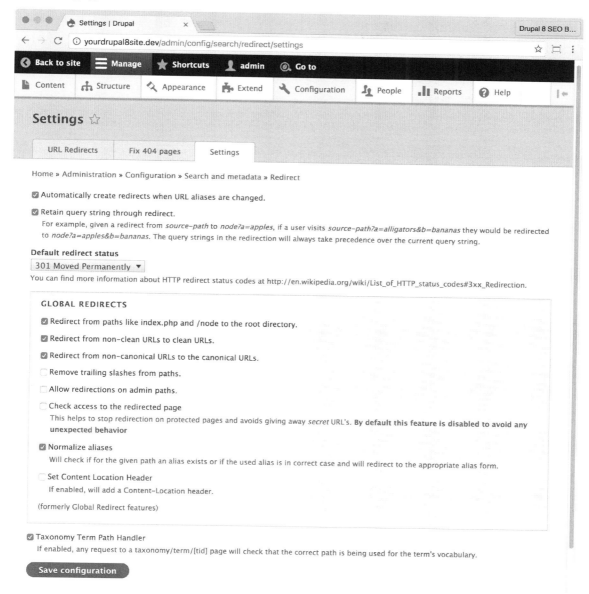

1. Visit the *Redirect* Admin page: Click **Manage > Configuration > Search and metadata > URL redirects > Settings** (Coffee: "url redirect" then click the Settings tab) or visit `http://yourDrupal8site.dev/admin/config/search/redirect/settings`.

2. Make sure your settings match the image above. These are the correct settings for most websites.

> A. Select the appropriate checkbox next to "Automatically create redirects when URL aliases are changed".
>
> B. Select the checkbox "Retain query string through redirect".
>
> C. Select "301 Moved Permanently" from the "Default redirect status" drop-down.
>
> D. Select the checkbox "Redirect from paths like index.php and /node to the root directory".
>
> E. Select the checkbox "Redirect from non-clean URLs to clean URLs."
>
> F. Select the checkbox "Redirect from non-canonical URLs to the canonical URLs".
>
> G. Select the checkbox "Normalize aliases".
>
> H. Select the checkbox "Taxonomy Term Path Handler".

3. If you changed anything, click the **Save configuration** button at the bottom of the page.

How to create a manual redirect

The *Redirect* module also allows you to create manual redirects. If you move content, put the wrong URL on some printed advertising, or you're migrating content, this is an invaluable function to understand.

> *Note: Creating a manual redirect isn't necessary right now. However, it's an essential skill for a growing site, so I'm covering it here.*

1. Go to the **URL Redirects** page: Click **Manage > Configuration > Search and metadata > URL redirects** (Coffee: "redirects") or visit
   `http://yourDrupal8site.dev/admin/config/search/redirect`.

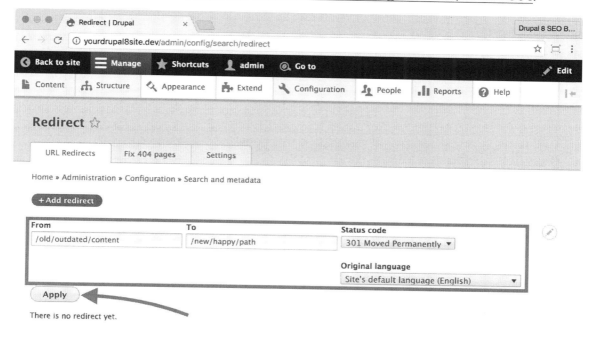

2. Enter the *From* and *To* URLs.

   A. "From" is the old URL that is broken.

   B. "To" is the new URL. If it's a link on your site, you can use just the path beginning with the /. For example: /your/path/here. If it's an external URL, put the entire URL including the http://.

3. Select "301 Moved Permanently" (or one of the other options as suited to the situation) from the *Status code* drop-down menu.

4. Set the "Original language" as appropriate.

5. Click the **Apply** button.

Now, when someone visits the old URL, they'll be automatically redirected to the new one.

The Pathauto Module

https://www.drupal.org/project/pathauto

The *Ctools* module is required: https://www.drupal.org/project/ctools

Credits & Thanks

Thank you to Mike Ryan (mikeryan on Drupal.org) for creating this module. Thank you to Greg Knaddison (greggles), Dave Reid, Sascha Grossenbacher (Berdir), and Freso for your contributions.

About the Pathauto Module

The *Pathauto* module generates URLs for your content without requiring you to enter the path alias manually. In other words, if the title of your new blog post is "My Big Cat" then *Pathauto* will set the URL to

`yourDrupal8site.dev/my-big-cat`

instead of

`yourDrupal8site.dev/node/23.`

Putting the right words in the URL is great for SEO, so this module is essential to your project. If you don't use the *Pathauto* module, you must remember to create every single content URL on your website manually.

> **SEO Training Camp**
> - *https://moz.com/learn/seo/url*
> - *https://www.drupal.org/documentation/modules/pathauto*
> - *https://www.drupal.org/documentation/modules/token*

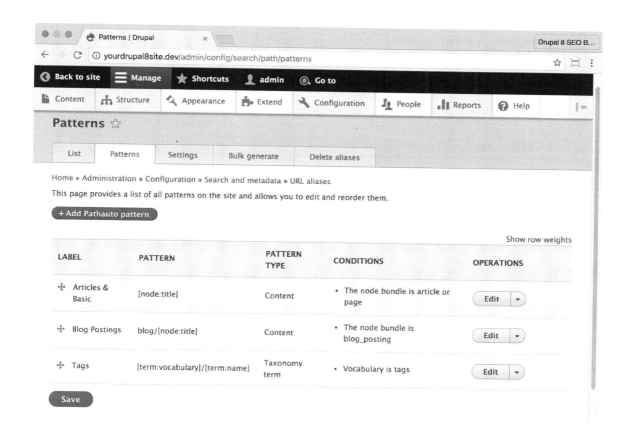

☐ *Install and Enable the Pathauto Module*

1. Install the *Pathauto* module and required *Ctools* module on your server. (See Chapter 1 for more instructions on installing modules.)

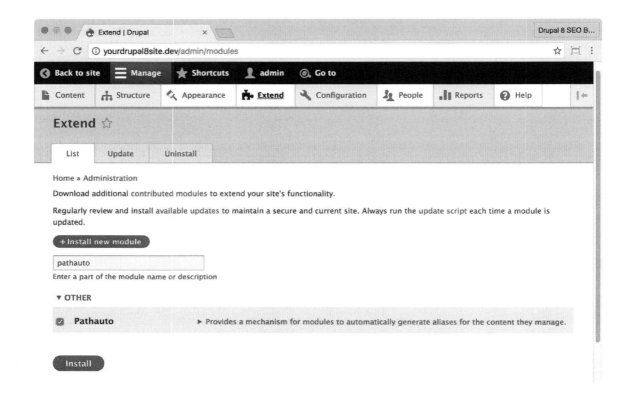

2. Go to the Extend page: Click **Manage > Extend** (Coffee: "extend") or visit `http://yourDrupal8site.dev/admin/modules`.

3. Select the checkbox next to *Pathauto* and click the **Install** button at the bottom of the page. You may get a message asking for your permission to install the *Ctools* module. If you do, click the **Continue** button.

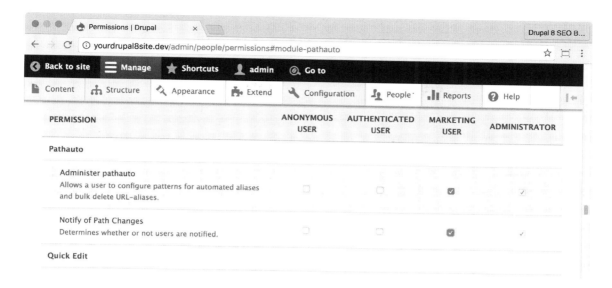

If necessary, give yourself permissions to use the *Pathauto* module.

1. Click **Manage > People > Permissions** (Coffee: "perm") or visit
   `http://yourDrupal8site.dev/admin/people/permissions`.

2. Select the appropriate checkboxes for

   - "Administer pathauto"
   - "Notify of Path Changes"

3. Click the **Save permissions** button at the bottom of the page.

☐ *Configure the Pathauto module*

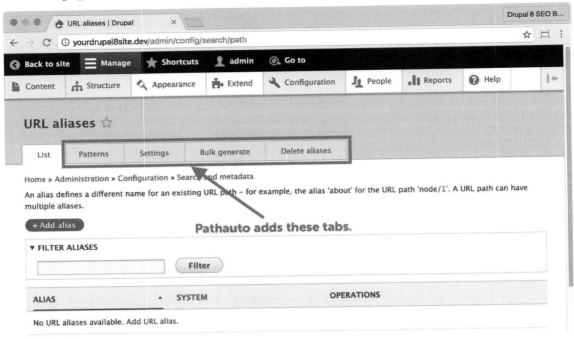

The *Pathauto* module adds four tabs to the *URL aliases* admin page. They are **Patterns**, **Settings**, **Bulk generate**, and **Delete aliases**. We only discuss **Patterns** and **Settings** in this book

> 1. Go to the *Pathauto* admin page: Click **Manage > Extend** (Coffee: "URL aliases") or visit
>
> http://yourDrupal8site.dev/admin/config/search/path/patterns.

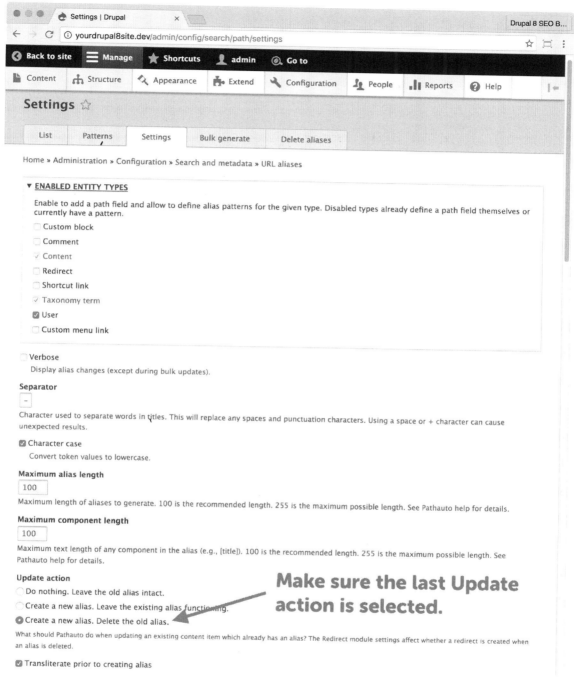

2. Click on **Settings**. The default settings are fine for most websites but check them to be sure that they haven't been changed. An important setting to double check is **Update action**. Ensure that **Create a new alias. Delete the old alias**. is selected.

3. If you changed anything, click the **Save configuration** button at the bottom of the page.

> *Note: If you change URLs a lot, you may want to select "Do nothing. Leave the old alias intact" instead. Redirects are OK for visitors but aren't great for rankings.*

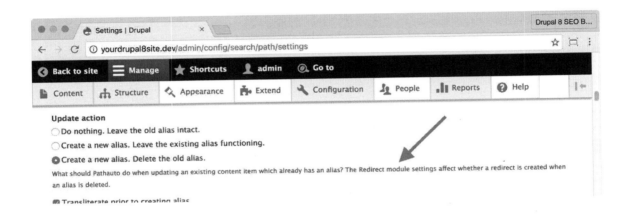

4. Click on the *Redirect* **module settings** link just below the **Update action** section or visit `https://yourDrupal8site.dev/admin/config/search/redirect/settings`.

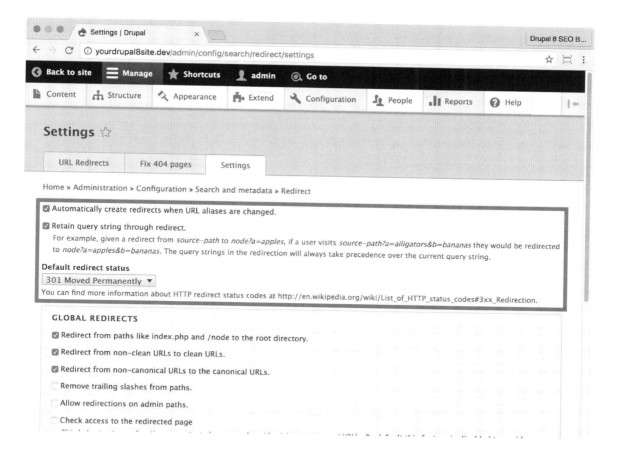

5. Update your settings to match those in the box above:

    A. Select "Automatically create redirects when URL aliases are changed".

    B. Select 'Retain query string through redirect".

    C. Set **Default redirect status** to "301 Moved Permanently".

> *Note: We'll investigate the rest of these settings in the next chapter.*

6. After any changes, be sure to click the **Save configuration** button at the bottom of the page.

A Brief Overview of the Token System

To fully take advantage of patterns, you need to understand a little about the *Token* system.

Tokens are variables in Drupal. There are thousands of Tokens available for you to use. To see what they are and get a better understanding of how they work you can visit http://yourDrupal8site.dev/admin/help/token.

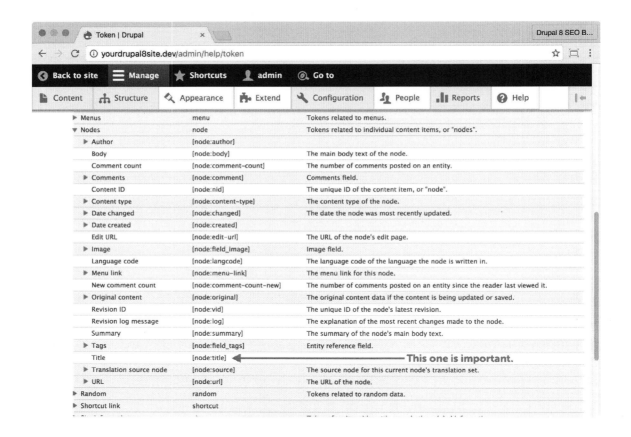

For now, we are going to focus on just a handful of critical Tokens that we'll use to create our URL path patterns. They are:

[node:title] - The title of the piece of content being displayed.

[term:vocabulary] - The vocabulary (top level category, so to speak) of the current term.

[term:name] - The name of the current term (bottom level category).

> **Key concept: Whenever Drupal sends a page to a visitor, it first replaces the tokens with the corresponding text. i.e. the "Today" token might be replaced with "February 22, 2017" or "August 26, 2018". Don't worry if this doesn't make sense yet. What you need to know right now is that we're going to tell Drupal to create some paths for us, and we're going to use Tokens to make it happen.**

☐ Create Pathauto Patterns

Drupal URL paths operate in patterns. Instead of creating a path to every single piece of content, it's better to specify a pattern (using tokens) for groups of content. Drupal will follow the pattern to create the path for each new piece of content, ensuring consistency across your website.

You're going to add a *Pathauto* pattern for each Content Type and taxonomy that you have.

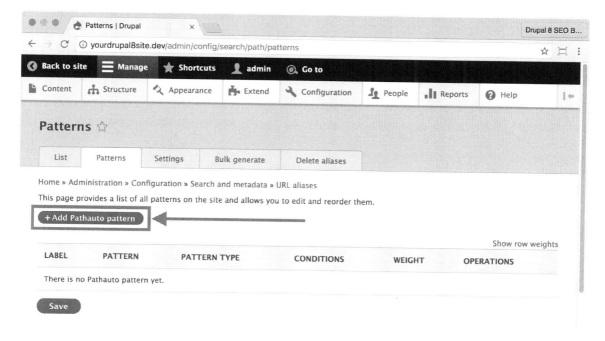

1. On the **URL alias > Pattern tab** (or visit
   http://yourDrupal8site.dev/admin/config/search/path/patterns)
   , click the **+ Add Pathauto pattern** button.

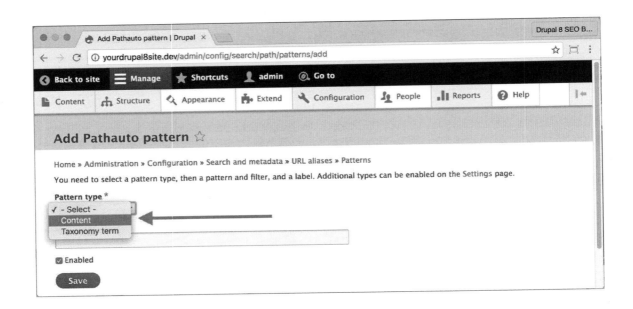

2. From the **Pattern type** drop-down, select *Content*. Several more fields
   will be displayed.

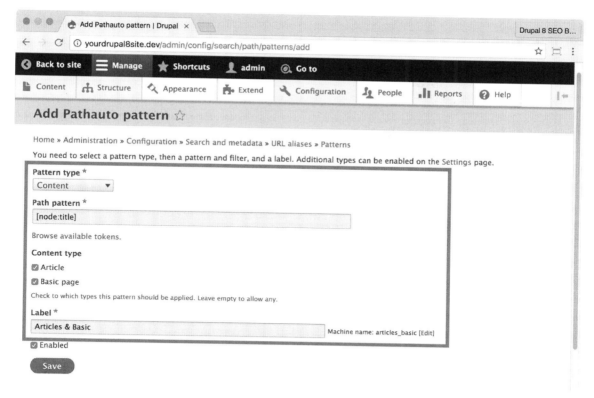

3. Fill out the fields as shown.

    A. **Path pattern**: "[node:title]"

    B. **Content type**: select "Article" and "Basic page"

    C. **Label**: Anything goes. I use the name of the Content Types: Articles & Basic

    D. Select the **Enabled** checkbox.

4. Click the **Save** button near the bottom of the page.

The resulting page will look something like this:

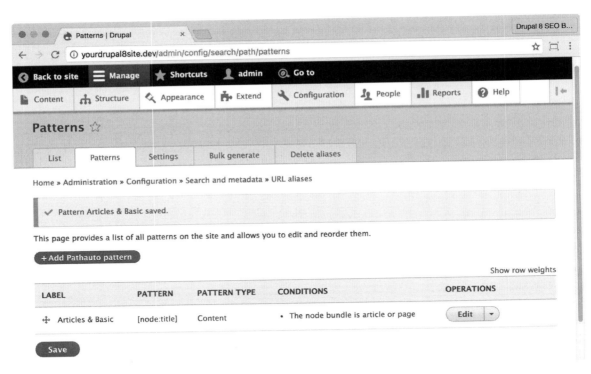

The [node:title] will be replaced with a normalized version of the title of the content. Drupal will turn the letters lowercase, replace spaces with dashes, and remove any odd characters.

> *Note: Remember the Settings tab we visited above? Most of that page is for setting the **Normalizing rules**. **Normalizing URLs is great for search engines, and so it's good for you, too.***

Congratulations! You've just created your first *Pathauto* pattern.

> 5. Repeat for each of your Content Types.

Going a step further with Pathauto

If you create your patterns like the example above, you will have a flat website with no hierarchy. If you created three basic pages called "Our Products", "Our Team", and "Our Customers" then you'd have three pages that look like this:

http://www.example.com/our-products

http://www.example.com/our-team

http://www.example.com/our-customers

Maybe that's what you want, but maybe you want something a little deeper. You can edit the patterns you've created or delete them and create new ones. For example, let's say you've created a new Content Type for your blog called *"Blog Postings"* and you want them to be under the /blog directory. You'd create a *Pathauto* pattern that looks like this:

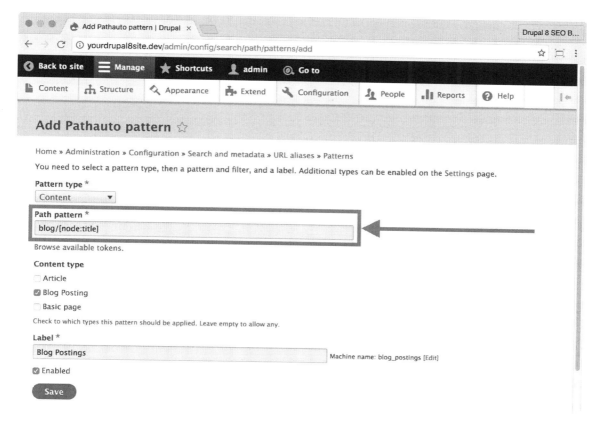

As you can see, you'd enter blog/[node:title] in the **Path pattern** field. Your blog URLs might look like this:

http://www.example.com/blog/my-happy-cat

http://www.example.com/blog/my-big-cat

http://www.example.com/blog/why-i-love-cats

Or, if your blog focuses on a single topic (*cats, is it?*) then you might put this:

`cat-blog/[node:title]`

Which produces this:

http://www.example.com/cat-blog/happy-cats

http://www.example.com/cat-blog/sad-cats

http://www.example.com/cat-blog/why-cats

Better! Now you've used the powerful key phrase "cat blog" which improves your SEO. Now, when you create each new piece of content, it will be in the `/cat-blog/` section of the website.

Now let's update your taxonomy terms. Let's say you create a new Pathauto pattern that looks like this:

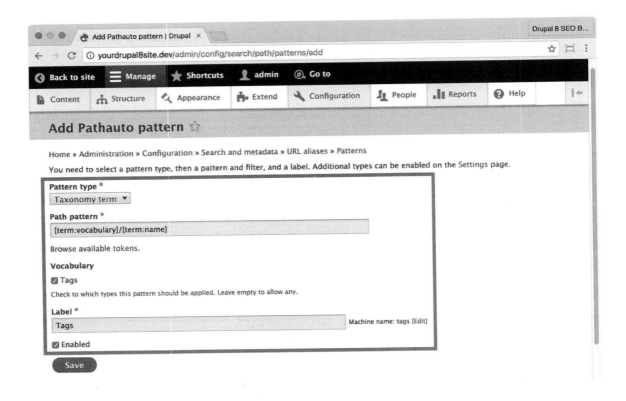

You might be wondering about the Path pattern for the Taxonomy term.

`[term:vocabulary]` is the top level category that the term belongs to. In this case, **Tags**.

`[term:name]` is the name of the tag, i.e. the tag itself.

In use, it might look like this:

http://www.example.com/tags/siamese

http://www.example.com/tags/persian

http://www.example.com/tags/abyssinian/

The Results

Below is a View that shows what the paths look like. This is fake content I created using the *Devel Generate* module:

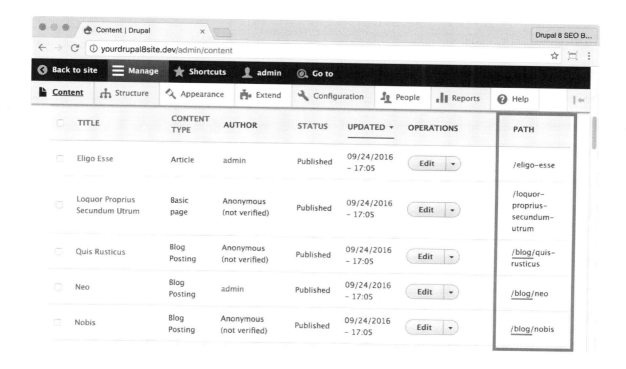

Notice that the blog path corresponds to its Content Type. This happened automatically now that the *Pathauto* module is configured properly.

Conclusion

In this chapter, we covered six essential *SEO Checklist* items including:

- You check your site for **Clean URLs**,
- You set up the ***Redirect*** module to redirect visitors to relevant pages, and
- You automated SEO-friendly URLs with the ***Pathauto*** module.

Your URLs are now enhancing your SEO. Your site shows the right content and link value is maintained even when your content changes. These are excellent steps to making Drupal 8 as effective as it can be.

In the next chapter, we'll continue down the *SEO Checklist* with a look at the ***Metatag*** and ***Alternate hreflang*** modules.

Chapter 4:
Basic SEO Part 2 — Metatags

*"This is a simple game. You throw the ball, you
hit the ball, you catch the ball. You got it?"*

"Skip"
BULL DURHAM

Items Covered

- *Metatag* module
- *Alternate hreflang* module
- Creating extra fields

IN MOST ENDEAVORS, you must excel at the basics before advanced techniques will work. It's true in sports, health, and certainly with SEO. In this chapter, we'll cover more of those basics including the all-important *Metatag* module and the *Alternate hreflang* module.

The Metatag Module

https://www.drupal.org/project/metatag

Credits & Thanks

Thank you to Dave Reid (Dave Reid on Drupal.org) for creating this module (and for his work on its predecessor.) Thank you to Damien McKenna (DamienMcKenna), Ivo Van Geertruyen (mr.baileys), Greg Knaddison (greggles), and a host of other developers for your contributions.

> *SEO Training Camp*
> - *Title tags: https://moz.com/learn/seo/title-tag*
> - *Meta tags: https://moz.com/blog/the-wonderful-world-of-seo-metatags*
> - *Metatag Module: https://dev.acquia.com/blog/drupal-8-module-of-the-week/drupal-8-module-of-the-week-metatag/17/02/2016/9716*

About the Metatag module

The *Metatag* module allows you to set up Drupal 8 to dynamically provide title tags and structured metadata, aka *meta tags*, on each page of your site.

Giving you control over your HTML **title tag** is the most important thing that the *Metatag* module does for SEO. That all-important tag is critical to your search engine ranking.

> Note: It may be confusing that the Title Tag functionality resides within the Metatag module, but it makes sense from a technical standpoint. Both the HTML title tag and meta tags are placed in the header of a web page. By handling them both in the Metatag module, it requires less code and enables (slightly) faster rendering of your web pages.

Besides handling the title tag, the *Metatag* module programmatically creates meta tags for your website. Meta tags are snippets of text that tell a search engine about your pages. Meta tags help your SEO by communicating clearly to the search engine and social networks what each page on your website is about and how you want them to describe it in the search results. If you don't do this, you will have to rely on the search engines to identify and classify your content. While they're kind of good at this, it's important enough that you don't want to leave it to chance.

☐ *Install and Enable the Metatag Module*

1. Install the *Metatag* module on your server. (See Chapter 1 for more instructions on installing modules.)

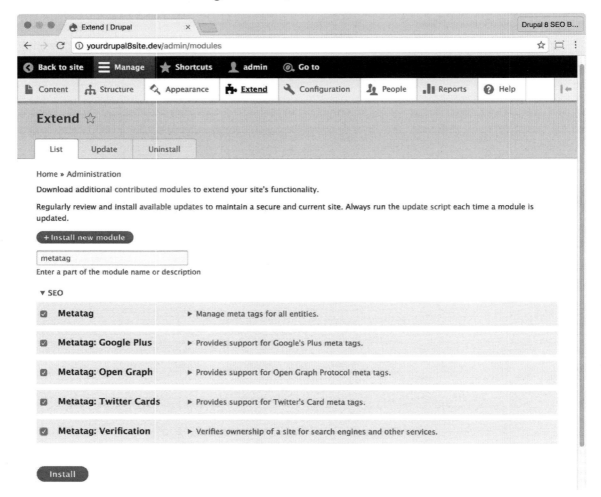

2. Go to the Extend page: Click **Manage > Extend** (Coffee: "extend") or visit `http://yourDrupal8site.dev/admin/modules`.

3. Select the checkboxes next to:

   • "Metatag"

   • "Metatag: Google Plus"

- 'Metatag: Open Graph'

- "Metatag: Twitter Cards"

- 'Verification'

4. Click the **Install** button at the bottom of the page. You may get a message asking for your permission to install the ***Token*** module. If you do, click the **Continue** button.

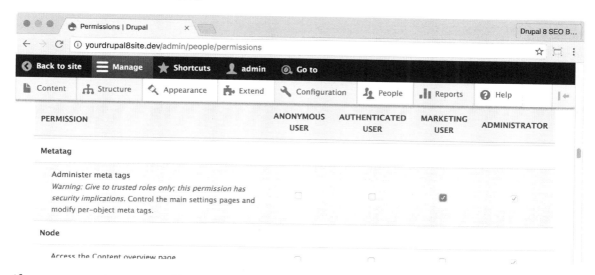

If necessary, give yourself permissions to use the *Metatag* module.

1. Click **Manage > People > Permissions** (Coffee: "perm") or visit `http://yourDrupal8site.dev/admin/people/permissions`.

2. Select the appropriate checkbox for "Administer Metatag".

3. Click the **Save permissions** button at the bottom of the page.

☐ Set Meta tags for your site

The *Metatag* module uses a series of inheritance. In other words, if a meta tag is not specified for a particular piece of content, the *Metatag* module will look higher in the hierarchy for a meta tag. If it doesn't find one at a higher level, it will not put that meta tag on the page.

The hierarchy looks something like this:

1. Global

    a. 403 Access Denied

    b. 404 Page Not Found

    c. Content

        i. Article

        ii. Basic Page

        iii. Blog Posting

    d. Front Page

    e. Taxonomy Term

        i. Category

        ii. Tags

    f. User

At the highest level are the Global meta tags. These are the default meta tags for your entire website. Every website section (such as content, sections, Taxonomies, etc.) will inherit these meta tags (unless you override them), so think carefully about what you enter here or you will create more work for yourself.

> *Tip: Like the* **Pathauto** *module, the* **Metatag** *module uses Tokens. Tokens are Drupal variables. You can insert them into your* **Metatag** *module, and Drupal will replace them with real text when the HTML page renders. For more information on Tokens, read Chapter 3.*

1. Click **Manage > Search and metadata > Metatag** (Coffee: "metatag") or visit `http://yourDrupal8site.dev/admin/config/search/metatag` in your browser.

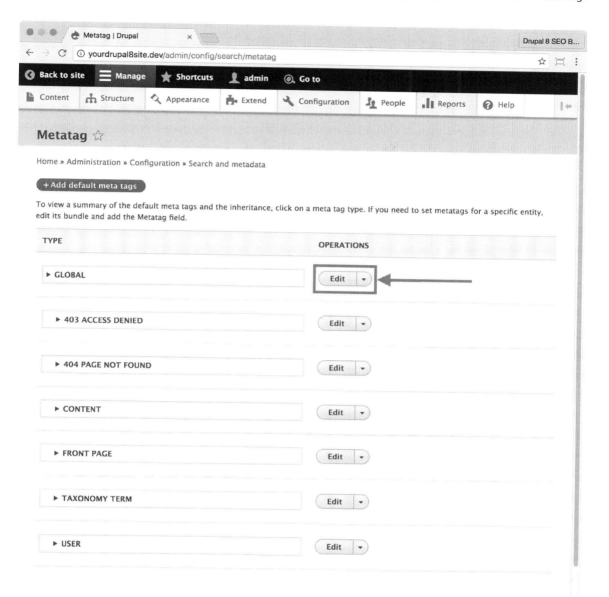

2. Click the **Edit** button next to **Global**.

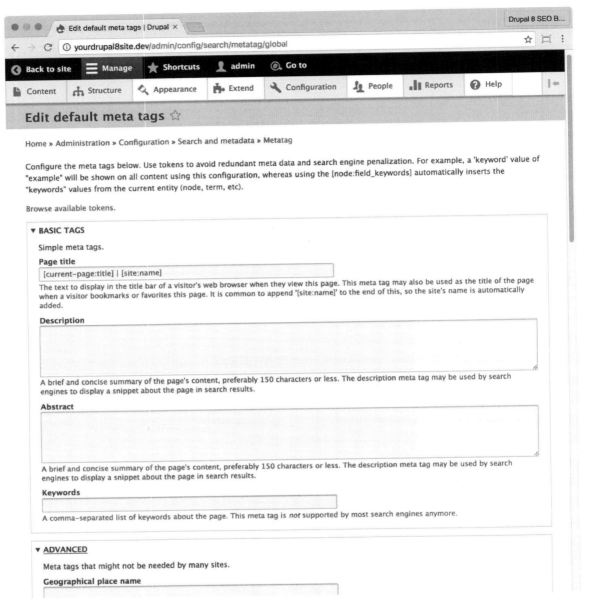

3. Use the chart below to edit the Global tags.

4. Click the **Save** button at the bottom of the page.

5. Return to the *Metatag* admin page (Coffee: metatag) and repeat steps 1-4 for **Front Page**, **Taxonomy Term**, **User**, and **Content**. The recommended settings for each type are below.

Global meta tags suggested settings

These will be the default meta tags for your website. Leave content-related meta tags like "description" or "image" blank. They may change based on Content Type. You'll configure them under "Content meta tags" below.

> Note: If a meta tag is not mentioned here, then leave it blank unless you have a particular reason to populate it with appropriate data.

Page title	`[current-page:title]	[site:name]`
Advanced Tags > Canonical URL	`[current-page:url:absolute]`
Advanced Tags > Shortlink URL	`[current-page:url:unaliased]`
Advanced Tags > Rights	*A copyright statement. i.e. "Copyright ©[date:html_year] My Corporation. All rights reserved."*
Advanced Tags > Referrer policy*	Unsafe URL
Open Graph > Site name	`[site:name]`
Open Graph > Page URL	`[current-page:url:absolute]`
Open Graph > Latitude	*Your Business' Latitude*
Open Graph > Longitude	*Your Business' Longitude*
Open Graph > Street Address	*Your Business' Street Address*
Open Graph > Locality	*Your Business' City*
Open Graph > Region	*Your Business' State or Region*
Open Graph > Postal/ZIP Code	*Your Business' Postal or ZIP Code*

Open Graph > Country name	*Your Business' Country name*
Open Graph > Email	*Your Business' Main Contact Email (i.e.,* `sales@volacci.com`*)*
Open Graph > Phone number	*Your Business' Primary Phone number*
Open Graph > Fax number	*Your Business' Fax number*
Open Graph > Locale	*Your Business' Locale* *Defaults to en_US. Find a full list here:* *https://msdn.microsoft.com/en-us/library/ee825488(v=cs.20).aspx*
Facebook > Admins	*The username of the Facebook admin for your business.*
Twitter Cards > Twitter card type	Summary Card
Twitter Cards > Site's Twitter account	*The username, with @ symbol, for your business. i.e.:* `@Volacci`
Twitter Cards > Site's Twitter account ID	*The Twitter account ID for your Business. Visit http://mytwitterid.com/ to find it.*

*Great confusion exists about **Referrer Policy**. In fact, the current description used by the Metatag module for this field is wrong! Referrer Policy is unrelated to follow or nofollow links. In reality, this field tells whether the referrer data will be passed when someone follows a link. In your Google Analytics reports you will see referrer data or it will say "Direct" if referrer data wasn't available. Ideally, everyone would use "Unsafe URL" and pass referrer data because it's useful for reporting where your traffic comes from.

> *SEO Training Camp*
> **https://moz.com/blog/meta-referrer-tag**

Front Page meta tags suggested settings

The front page of your website is incredibly important. Take some extra care to get this one just perfect. Several fields that would have been prepopulated are overridden with more appropriate content.

> *Note: If a meta tag is not mentioned here, then it is inherited from the Global meta tag setting. It should be left blank unless you have a particular reason to override it with appropriate data.*

Basic Tags > Page title	*The title tag for your front page. Usually something like "'key phrase' by Company"*
Basic Tags > Description	*The description tag for your home page.*
Basic Tags > Abstract	*The description tag for your home page.*
Basic Tags > Keywords	*Put one obvious keyword here. No more, no less. The Keywords meta tag has no value to most search engines so don't waste time on it.*
Advanced > Canonical URL	`[site:url]`
Advanced > Image	**The full URL to your website's logo.*
Open Graph > Site name	`[site:name]`
Open Graph > Content type	Website
Open Graph > Page URL	`[site:url]`
Open Graph > Title	`[site:name]`
Open Graph > Description	*The description tag for your home page.*

Open Graph > Image	*The full URL to your website's logo.
Open Graph > Image type	The type of image from Open Graph > Image. Use 'image/gif', 'image/jpeg' or 'image/png'.
Open Graph > Image width	*Open Graph > Image width in pixels.
Open Graph > Image height	*Open Graph > Image width in pixels.
Google Plus > Name	`[site:name]`
Google Plus > Description	The description tag for your home page.
Google Plus > Image	*The full URL to your website's logo.
Twitter Cards > Description	The description tag for your home page.
Twitter Cards > Title	`[site:name]`
Twitter Cards > Page URL	`[site:url]`
Twitter Cards > Image URL	Same as Advanced > Image
Twitter Cards > Image height	*Twitter Cards > Image URL height in pixels.
Twitter Cards > Image width	*Twitter Cards > Image URL width in pixels.
Twitter Cards > App Info (several fields)	Include this information if your company has an app.

*Warning: Use your company logo as the image for the home page only! Avoid using the site logo as the image on the rest of your pages.

> *Tip: Tokens don't exist for image width and height so you'll only enter this information for your front page if the image never changes. Otherwise, leave them blank.*

Taxonomy term meta tag settings

Some fields that would have been prepopulated are overridden with more appropriate content.

> **Note: If a meta tag is not mentioned here, then it is inherited from the Global meta tag setting. It should be left blank unless you have a particular reason to override it with appropriate data.**

Basic Tags > Page title	[term:name] | [site:name]
Basic Tags > Description	[term:description]
Basic Tags > Abstract	[term:description]
Basic Tags > Keywords	[term:name]
Open Graph > Title	[term:name] | [site:name]
Open Graph > Description	[term:description]
Google Plus > Name	[term:name] | [site:name]
Google Plus > Description	[term:description]
Twitter Cards > Description	[term:description]
Twitter Cards > Title	[term:name] | [site:name]

User meta tag settings

Some fields that would have been prepopulated are overridden with more appropriate content.

> **Note: If a meta tag is not mentioned here, then it is inherited from the Global meta tag setting. It should be left blank unless you have a particular reason to override it with appropriate data.**

Basic Tags > Page title	`[user:name] on [site:name]`
Basic Tags > Keywords	`[user:name]`
Open Graph > Title	`[user:name] on [site:name]`
Google Plus > Name	`[user:name] on [site:name]`
Twitter Cards > Title	`[user:name] on [site:name]`

Why use "on" instead of "|" as a separator when creating User meta tags? Because that's a common way to search for somebody's profile on a particular website. Go ahead and try these searches:

- Ben Finklea on Twitter.com
- Ben Finklea on Drupal.org
- Ben Finklea on Volacci.com
- Ben Finklea on LinkedIn.com

Content meta tags suggested settings

Your Content Types—and thus your content—fall under the Content meta tag category. While your specific settings may vary, I've found these to work well for many sites. Some fields that would have been prepopulated are overridden with more appropriate content.

> **Note: If a meta tag is not mentioned here, then it is inherited from the Global meta tag setting. It should be left blank unless you have a particular reason to override it with appropriate data.**

Basic Tags > Page title	`[node:title] | [site:name]`
Basic Tags > Description	`[node:summary]`
Basic Tags > Abstract	`[node:summary]`
Open Graph > Content type	`article`
Open Graph > Title	`[node:title] | [site:name]`
Open Graph > Description	`[node:summary]`
Open Graph > Image*	`[node:field_image]`
Open Graph > Content modification date & time	`[node:changed:custom:c]`
Open Graph > Article publication date & time	`[node:created:custom:c]`
Open Graph > Article modification date & time	`[node:changed:custom:c]`
Google Plus > Name	`[node:title] |`

	[site:name]
Google Plus > Description	[node:summary]
Google Plus > Image*	[node:field_image]
Twitter Cards > Description	[node:summary]
Twitter Cards > Title	[node:title] | [site:name]
Twitter Cards > Image URL*	[node:field_image]

Tip: There may be many image fields depending on how your site is set up. You can include multiple fields by separating them with a comma. Like this:
`[node:field_image], [node:field_image_thumbnail], [node:field_header_image],` *etc.*

Create separate meta tags for each Content Type

There are many reasons that you may not want to populate certain meta tags on every Content Type automatically. For example, you may not want your company's product pages associated with an individual's Twitter account (**Twitter Cards > Creator's Twitter account**) just because they created the node. When a blog is posted, on the other hand, it is a very good idea to include the writer's Twitter Card meta data.

When you get down to specific Content Types, it's impossible for a book like this one to tell you how to set everything up. Drupal's tremendous flexibility allows the creation of the Content Types that make the most sense to you. Here are some of the most common ones and you can figure things out from there.

First, we're going to need some extra fields to hold data that we'll need for our meta tags.

Create Additional Contact Fields for Meta tags

You'll need to create some additional contact fields to store contact information (like Twitter handle or Facebook username) for your bloggers. The ease in which you can create more contact fields elevates Drupal 8 over other platforms and earlier versions. Delete that email to your developer! You can do this yourself.

These fields will store the few bits of extra data that you will need to create meta tags or display on the visible portions of your user pages.

1. Click **Manage > Configuration > People > Account Settings > Manage Fields** (Coffee: "fields") or visit
   ```
   http://yourDrupal8site.dev/admin/config/people/accounts
   /fields.
   ```

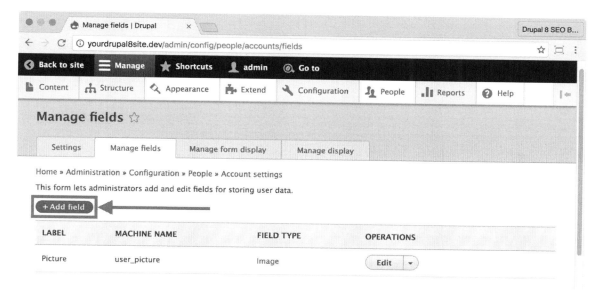

2. Click the **+Add field** button.

3. Fill out the fields.

   A. Under **Add a new field** select "Text (plain)".

   B. For **Label**, enter `Twitter Handle`.

4. Click the **Save and continue** button at the bottom of the page.

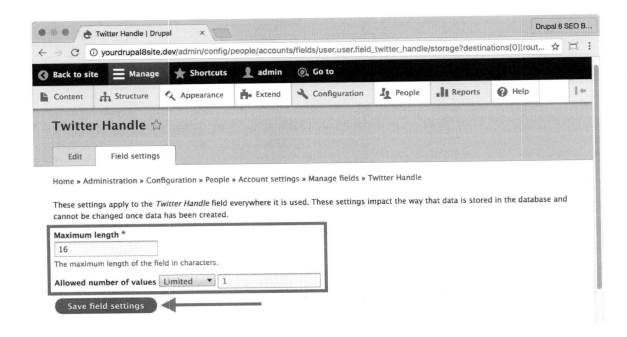

5. Fill out the fields.

A. For **Maximum length** enter 16, This is the maximum length of a Twitter handle (15) plus an extra for the @ symbol.

B. For **Allowed number of values**, leave the defaults of "Limited" and "1".

6. Click the **Save field settings** button.

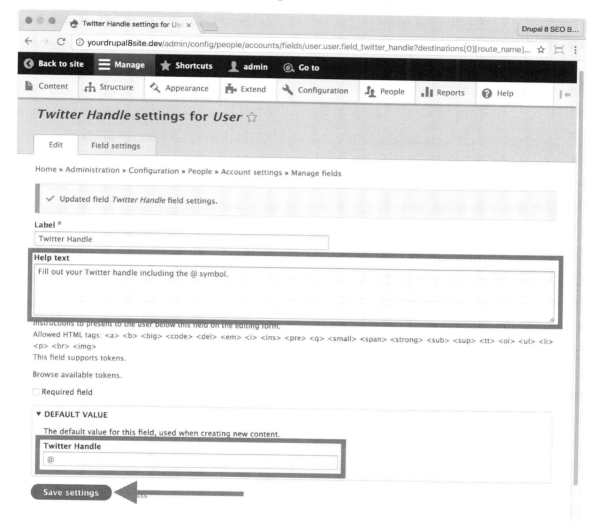

7. On the final screen, under **Help text** enter "Fill out your Twitter handle including the @ symbol."

8. Set the Default Value to "@". This will help users to understand what they should put in the field.

9. Click the **Save settings** button.

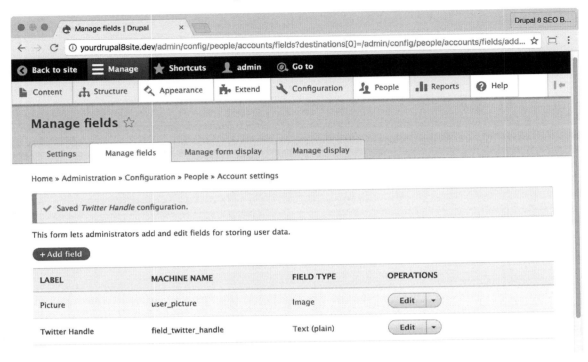

10. Repeat these steps for the following fields using the same settings as above with the changes detailed below. They are all "Text (plain)" fields, use the following name and maximum length.

> A. **Twitter account number** - 16 characters
>
> B. **Google+ account name** - 21 characters
>
> C. **LinkedIn URL** - 100 characters
>
> D. **Facebook account name** - 75 characters

11. Add any more social accounts you use. Pinterest, Baido, Instagram, Drupal.org, etc.

You can see the profile fields that you've added when you edit a user account. If you're logged in, go to `http://yourDrupal8site.dev/user` and then click **Edit**.

Fill them out for each user (including yourself) who will be creating content on your website. In the next section, you'll use those fields in your meta tags. When you view a user page, they'll look something like this:

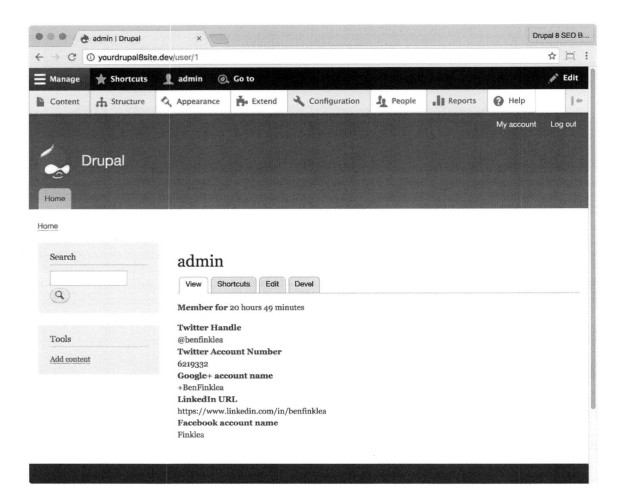

Your developer can style them to look exactly how you want. You can even include social icons or a stream of your recent posts. For meta tag purposes, however, we just need the text.

Break out meta tags for each Content Type

If you want separate meta tags for each Content Type, you've got to break out each one.

1. Go to **Manage > Configuration > Search and Metadata > Metatags** (Coffee: metatag).

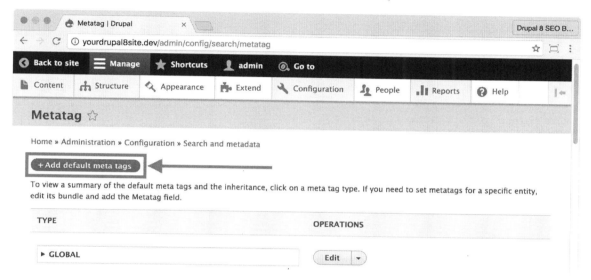

2. Click the **+Add default meta tags** button.

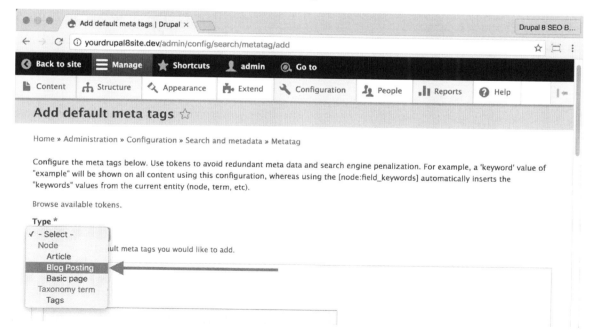

3. From the **Type** drop-down field, select **Node > Blog Posting** (this name will vary based upon what you've called your Blog Content Type).

4. Set default meta tags for the Content Type. *See charts below.*

5. Click the **Save** button near the bottom of the page.

Blog Posting meta tags suggested settings

Notice that there are few settings. If a particular meta tag is not mentioned here, then it is inherited from the Global meta tag settings or the Content meta tag settings.

> *Note: Unless specified below, leave fields blank unless you have a particular reason to override it with appropriate data. Some fields below purposefully override previous settings.*

Open Graph > Article author	`https://www.facebook.com/[node:author:field_facebook_account_name]`
Twitter Cards > Creator's Twitter account	`[node:author:field_twitter_handle]`
Twitter Cards > Creator's Twitter account ID	`[node:author:field_twitter_account_number]`

Article meta tags suggested settings

Use these settings if you use Articles as content that are individually written and attributed to a single person. Do not use these settings if you use Articles as general site content.

Open Graph > Article author	`https://www.facebook.com/[node:author:field_facebook_account_name]`
Twitter Cards > Creator's Twitter account	`[node:author:field_twitter_handle]`
Twitter Cards > Creator's Twitter account ID	`[node:author:field_twitter_account_number]`

Basic page meta tags suggested settings

No more settings are required.

Test Open Graph tags

Facebook provides a testing tool for Open Graph tags called "Sharing Debugger". It will tell you if you've configured your Open Graph tags correctly and it will let you know other ways to improve your website. Go to https://developers.facebook.com/tools/debug/ for more information.

Alternate Hreflang module

https://www.drupal.org/project/hreflang

Credit and Thanks

Thank you to Mark Burdett (mfb on Drupal.org) for creating and maintaining this module.

About Alternate Hreflang module

The *Alternate hreflang* module automatically adds hreflang tags to your pages. Search engines reference the alternate hreflang tag to serve the correct language or regional URL in search results which is important for multilingual websites.

In Drupal 8, the Core Content Translation module does already add hreflang tags to translated entity pages. Hreflang tags should be added to all pages, even untranslated ones. This module takes care of this for you.

☐ *Install and Enable the Alternate hreflang module*

1. Install the *Alternate hreflang* module on your server. (See Chapter 1 for more instructions on installing modules.)

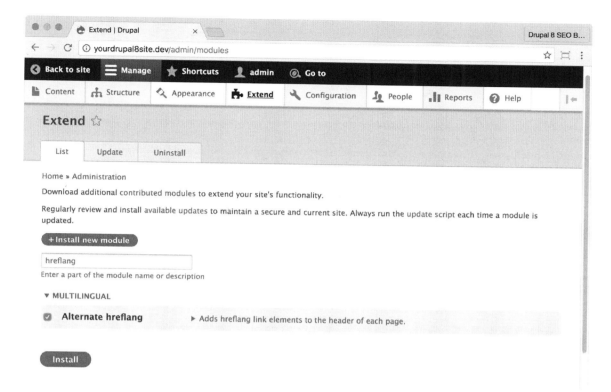

2. Go to the Extend page: Click **Manage > Extend** (Coffee: "extend") or visit `http://yourDrupal8site.dev/admin/modules`.

3. Select the checkbox next to "Alternate hreflang" and click the **Install** button at the bottom of the page.

There are no permissions to set or further settings to change.

As you can see from the above screenshot in the example website, the `hreflang` for each different language version of the site has been set by the *Alternate Hreflang* module.

Conclusion

In this chapter we covered three important *SEO Checklist* items related to your meta tags:

- You set up your site-wide meta tags and title tags using the **Metatag** module, and
- you made sure that non-translated pages had their proper tag using the **Alternate hreflang** module.

By completing these items, you ensured that you're communicating clearly with Google, Facebook, and Twitter about each page of content on your site using meta tags. This is a major step to proper SEO.

In the next chapter, we'll continue down the *SEO Checklist* and set up the **XML Sitemap** module, authenticate your website with the major search engines and install the **Google Analytics** module.

Chapter 5: Search Engines

"Help me...help you!"

Jerry Maguire
JERRY MAGUIRE

Items Covered

- XML Sitemap module
- Cron
- Google Account and Google site authentication
- Microsoft Live ID and Bing site authentication
- XML sitemap and the `robots.txt` file
- Google Analytics module

LIKE AGENT JERRY MAGUIRE'S EMOTIONAL PLEA to self-aggrandizing wide receiver Rod Tidwell in the movie *Jerry Maguire*, the search engines are crying "help me help you!". They want you to help them crawl and index your website properly. They provide tools and reports to help you communicate with them and better understand what's going on with your websites.

This chapter will help you set up your website to communicate well with the search engines. You'll create search engine accounts, build sitemaps, authenticate (provide proof of site ownership), and submit your website's content to the search engines.

The XML Sitemap Module

https://www.drupal.org/project/xmlsitemap

> *Warning: I've had some trouble getting the XML Sitemap module to work on some websites. In those cases, I used the* **Simple XML Sitemap** *module which works great but lacks some of the robustness:*
> *https://www.drupal.org/project/simple_sitemap.*

Credits & Thanks

Thank you to Darren Oh (Darren Oh on Drupal.org) for creating this module.

Thank you Dave Reid (Dave Reid), Andrei Mateescu (amateescu), Andrei Dincu (andrei.dincu), Juampy NR (juampynr), and many others for your contributions to the *XML Sitemap* module.

> *SEO Training Camp*
> *https://moz.com/beginners-guide-to-seo/search-engine-tools-and-services*

About the XML Sitemap module

The *XML Sitemap* module creates an *XML Sitemap* of your content that you can submit to the search engines. An **XML sitemap** is a specially-formatted summary of each piece of content on your website. You can read more at http://www.sitemaps.org/.

> *Tip: If you're running an eCommerce website, this module is of particular importance. I've seen catalogs with extensive product listings increase traffic by thousands of visitors per day with an XML sitemap.*

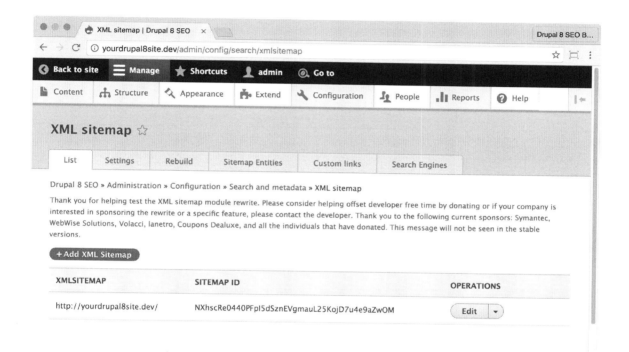

Having an XML sitemap helps your SEO by giving Google a list of the pages that you wish them to crawl. While Google *can* crawl your site without an XML sitemap, bigger and more complex sites confuse the crawler so it could potentially miss pages and even whole sections. If you don't do this, you will have to manually submit every single page of your site to Google which is ridiculously time-consuming.

☐ *Install and Enable the XML Sitemap Module*

1. Install the ***XML Sitemap*** module on your server. (See Chapter 1 for more instructions on installing modules.)

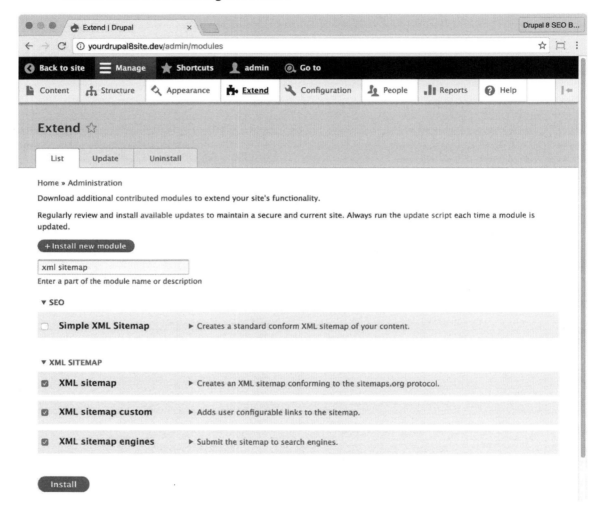

2. Go to the Extend page: Click **Manage > Extend** (Coffee: "extend") or visit `http://yourDrupal8site.dev/admin/modules`.

3. Select the checkbox next to "XML sitemap", "XML sitemap custom", and "XML sitemap engines" and click the **Install** button at the bottom of the page.

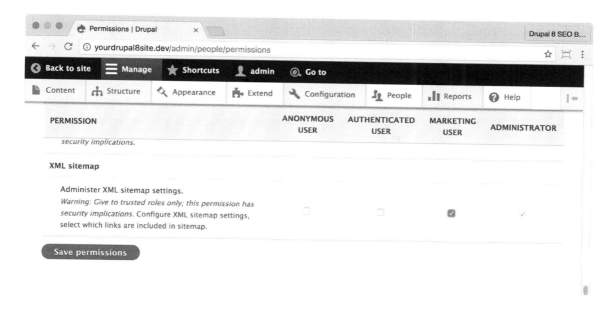

If necessary, give yourself permissions to use the *XML Sitemap* module.

1. Click **Manage > People > Permissions** (Coffee: "perm") or visit
   `http://yourDrupal8site.dev/admin/people/permissions`.

2. Select the appropriate checkbox for "Administer XML sitemap settings".

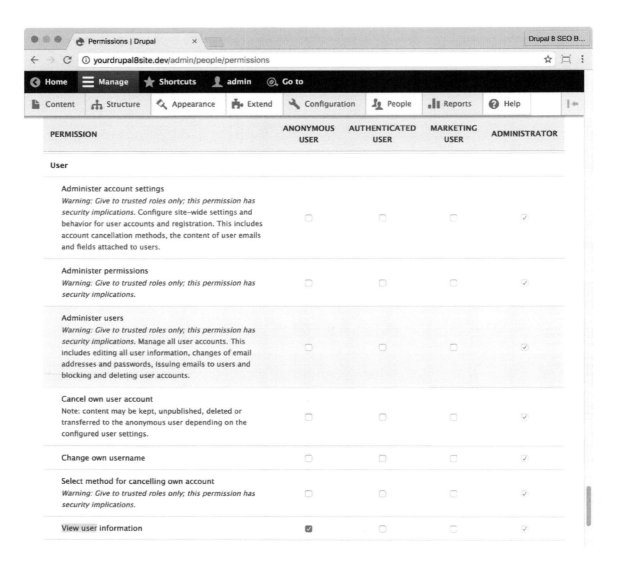

3. Select the appropriate checkbox for "User > View user information" if you wish for your XML sitemap to include user information.

4. Click the **Save permissions** button at the bottom of the page.

☐ *Configure the XML Sitemap module*

1. Click **Manage > Configuration > Search and metadata > XML Sitemap** (Coffee: "xml", then click the **Entities** tab) or visit

```
http://yourDrupal8site.dev/admin/config/search/xmlsitem
ap/entities/settings).
```

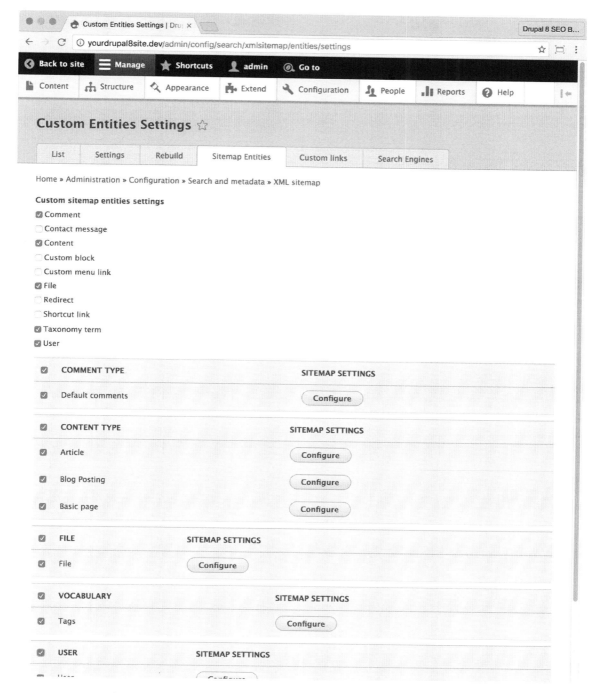

2. Select the checkbox next to the entities that you want to show up in Google. You will likely select your Content Types and Taxonomies but you may

or may not want to select "Comments", "User", or other items. If in doubt, include them as they're often good content for SEO purposes.

3. Click the **Save** button at the bottom of the page.

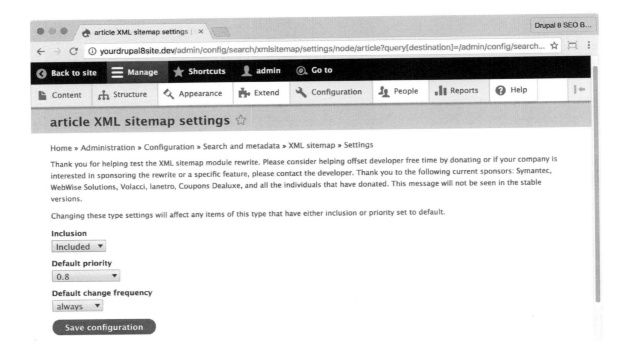

4. Click the **Configure** button next to "Article".

    A. **Inclusion** set to "Included".

    B. **Default priority** set to "0.8".

    C. **Default change frequency** set to "always".

    D. Click the **Save configuration** button at the bottom of the page.

5. Do the same for **Blog postings** and your other primary Content Types.

6. Leave the rest of the **Entity Sitemap Settings** on their defaults.

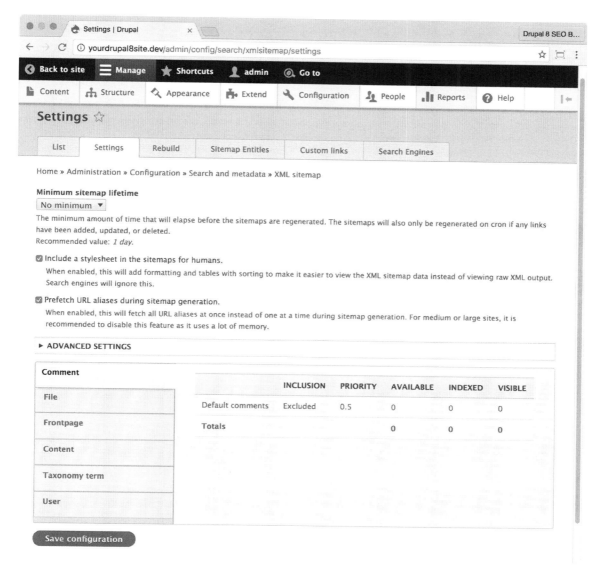

7. Now, click the *XML sitemap* **Settings** tab to go to `http://`
`yourDrupal8site.dev/admin/config/search/xmlsitemap/settings`.

8. Set Minimum sitemap lifetime to "No minimum".

9. Select the **Include a stylesheet** checkbox.

10. Prefetch URL aliases set as follows:

   A. Small sites (less than 500 nodes) — select the checkbox.

   B. Medium or large sites (more than 500 nodes) — unselect the checkbox.

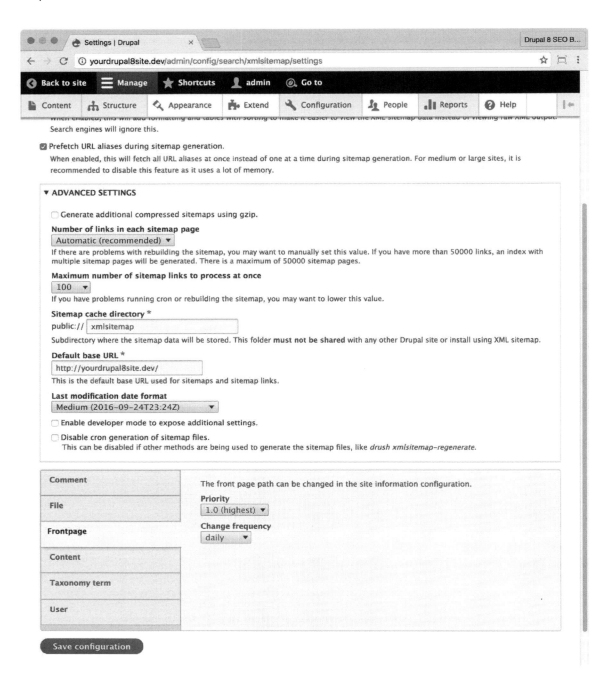

11. Leave the settings under the **Advanced Settings** as shown in the screenshot here.

12. Click the **Save Configuration** button at the bottom of the page.

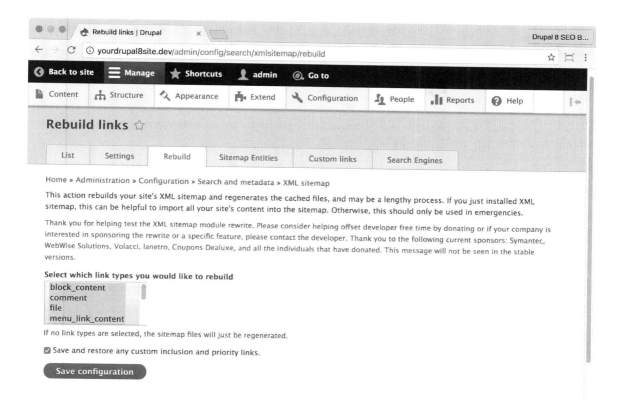

13. Select the **Rebuild** tab (http://yourDrupalsite.com/admin/config/search/xmlsitemap/rebuild)

14. Select all the items in the menu and make sure the "Save and restore any custom inclusions and priority links." is checked.

15. Click **Save configuration** to generate your sitemap for the first time.

The XML sitemap is automatically updated when Cron runs. That makes it unnecessary to rebuild your sitemap again unless you run into problems.

☐ **Set up Cron**

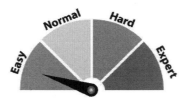

Cron is a system built into your server that runs maintenance tasks on a regular basis. The Drupal cron tasks maintain and clean up your Drupal site. It does things like check for updates, indexes content, and rebuilds XML sitemaps.

1. Click **Manage > Configuration > System > Cron** (Coffee: "cron") or visit `http://yourDrupal8site.dev/admin/config/system/cron` in your browser.

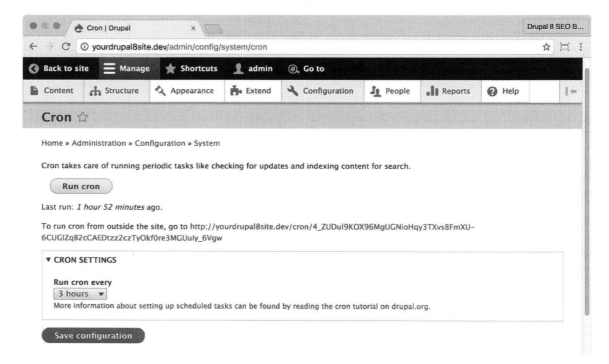

2. Set **Run cron every** to "3 hours". You can set this to be more frequent or less frequent depending on how often you update your website.

3. Click the **Save configuration** button at the bottom of the page.

Now your XML sitemap will stay up to date with your site content.

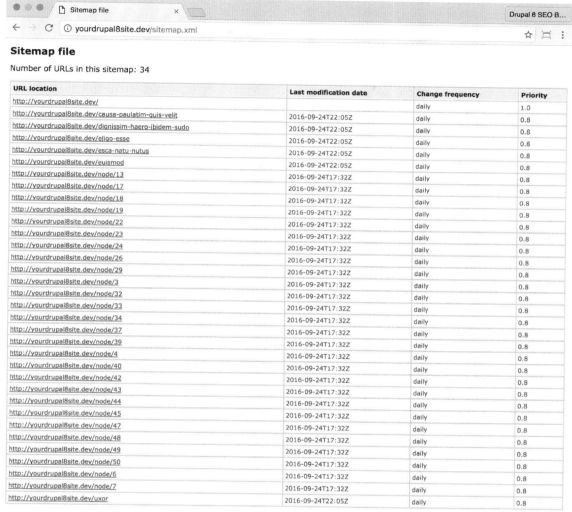

URL location	Last modification date	Change frequency	Priority
http://yourdrupal8site.dev/		daily	1.0
http://yourdrupal8site.dev/causa-paulatim-quis-velit	2016-09-24T22:05Z	daily	0.8
http://yourdrupal8site.dev/dignissim-haero-ibidem-sudo	2016-09-24T22:05Z	daily	0.8
http://yourdrupal8site.dev/eligo-esse	2016-09-24T22:05Z	daily	0.8
http://yourdrupal8site.dev/esca-natu-nutus	2016-09-24T22:05Z	daily	0.8
http://yourdrupal8site.dev/euismod	2016-09-24T22:05Z	daily	0.8
http://yourdrupal8site.dev/node/13	2016-09-24T17:32Z	daily	0.8
http://yourdrupal8site.dev/node/17	2016-09-24T17:32Z	daily	0.8
http://yourdrupal8site.dev/node/18	2016-09-24T17:32Z	daily	0.8
http://yourdrupal8site.dev/node/19	2016-09-24T17:32Z	daily	0.8
http://yourdrupal8site.dev/node/22	2016-09-24T17:32Z	daily	0.8
http://yourdrupal8site.dev/node/23	2016-09-24T17:32Z	daily	0.8
http://yourdrupal8site.dev/node/24	2016-09-24T17:32Z	daily	0.8
http://yourdrupal8site.dev/node/26	2016-09-24T17:32Z	daily	0.8
http://yourdrupal8site.dev/node/29	2016-09-24T17:32Z	daily	0.8
http://yourdrupal8site.dev/node/3	2016-09-24T17:32Z	daily	0.8
http://yourdrupal8site.dev/node/32	2016-09-24T17:32Z	daily	0.8
http://yourdrupal8site.dev/node/33	2016-09-24T17:32Z	daily	0.8
http://yourdrupal8site.dev/node/34	2016-09-24T17:32Z	daily	0.8
http://yourdrupal8site.dev/node/37	2016-09-24T17:32Z	daily	0.8
http://yourdrupal8site.dev/node/39	2016-09-24T17:32Z	daily	0.8
http://yourdrupal8site.dev/node/4	2016-09-24T17:32Z	daily	0.8
http://yourdrupal8site.dev/node/40	2016-09-24T17:32Z	daily	0.8
http://yourdrupal8site.dev/node/42	2016-09-24T17:32Z	daily	0.8
http://yourdrupal8site.dev/node/43	2016-09-24T17:32Z	daily	0.8
http://yourdrupal8site.dev/node/44	2016-09-24T17:32Z	daily	0.8
http://yourdrupal8site.dev/node/45	2016-09-24T17:32Z	daily	0.8
http://yourdrupal8site.dev/node/47	2016-09-24T17:32Z	daily	0.8
http://yourdrupal8site.dev/node/48	2016-09-24T17:32Z	daily	0.8
http://yourdrupal8site.dev/node/49	2016-09-24T17:32Z	daily	0.8
http://yourdrupal8site.dev/node/50	2016-09-24T17:32Z	daily	0.8
http://yourdrupal8site.dev/node/6	2016-09-24T17:32Z	daily	0.8
http://yourdrupal8site.dev/node/7	2016-09-24T17:32Z	daily	0.8
http://yourdrupal8site.dev/uxor	2016-09-24T22:05Z	daily	0.8

Generated by the Drupal XML sitemap module.

To view your XML sitemap, visit http://yourDrupal8site.dev/sitemap.xml.

In the next few sections, we'll submit your newly created XML sitemap to Google and Bing.

Submit your site to Google

☐ *Get a Google Account*

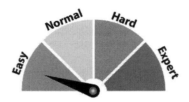

An account with Google is a gateway to many excellent tools offered by the world's largest search engine. You will get access to:

- **Google Search Console** (previously known as **Google Webmaster Tools**)—a free web service for webmasters. It allows you to check indexing status and optimize visibility of your websites.
- **Google Analytics**—a free web analytics service that tracks and reports website traffic, sources, usage, and more.
- **Google Adwords Keyword Planner**—a free keyword research tool that allows you to see how many times words and phrases are searched in Google.
- and much more.

If you don't already have one, sign up for free at

https://accounts.google.com/SignUp

☐ *Verify with Google Search Console*

By verifying your website, you prove to Google that you own that domain. Then, Google will accept your XML sitemap and start sending you alerts if there are any issues with your site.

> *Note: Verify your live, production website. Do not verify your development or staging sites.*

1. Sign-in to **Google Search Console** at https://www.google.com/webmasters/.

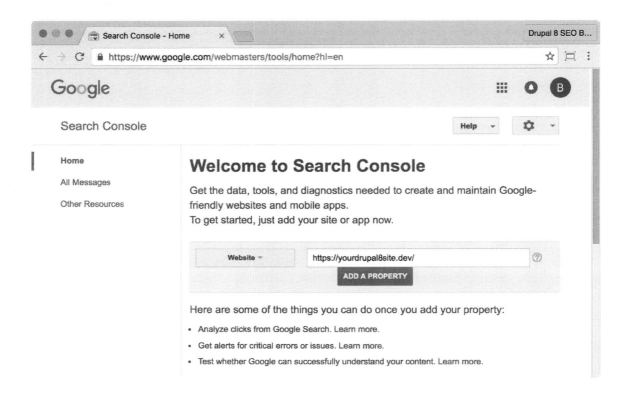

2. Put your website's URL in the field provided. If you use HTTPS, be sure to include the "s" as Google treats them as two separate sites.

3. Click the red **Add a Property** button.

4. You can authenticate with your Domain Name provider. Often, that option is challenging and time-consuming. Fortunately, there are easier methods available.

5. Click the **Alternate methods** tab.

6. Select the **HTML tag** radio button.

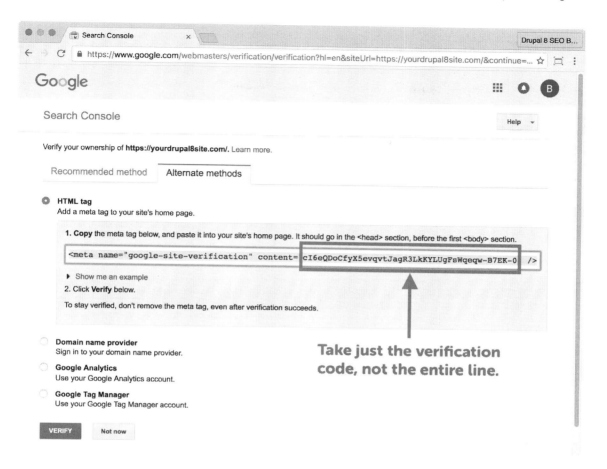

7. Copy just the content part of the meta tag from the page. You may need to copy the entire line into a text editor and then copy the code. The piece you need looks something like this:

```
cI6eQDoCfyX5evqvtJagR3LkKYLUgFsWqeqw-B7EK-0
```

8. On your Drupal 8 site go to **Manage > Configuration > Search and metadata > Metatag** (Coffee: "metatag") or visit

```
http://yourDrupal8site.dev/admin/config/search/metatag
```
in your browser.

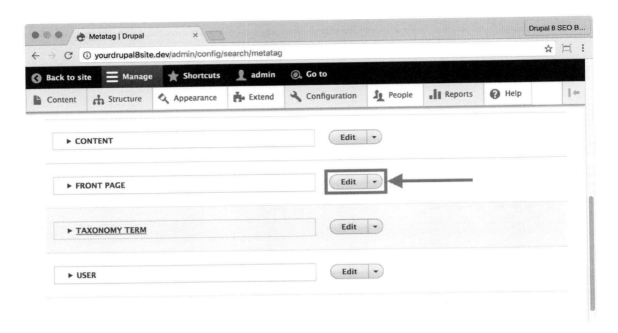

9. Click the **Edit** button next to "Front Page".

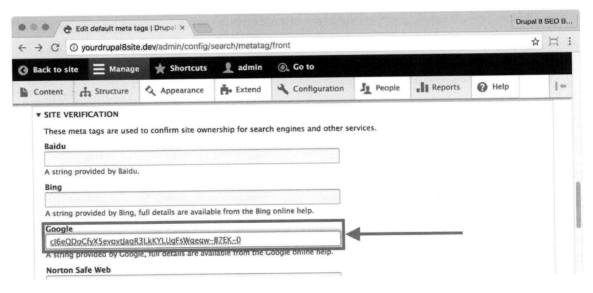

10. Under **Site Verification** > **Google**, paste in the meta tag copied from **Google Search Console**.

11. Click the **Save** button at the bottom of the page.

12. Go to **Admin** > **Configuration** > **Performance** (Coffee: "performance"). Click the **Clear all caches** button.

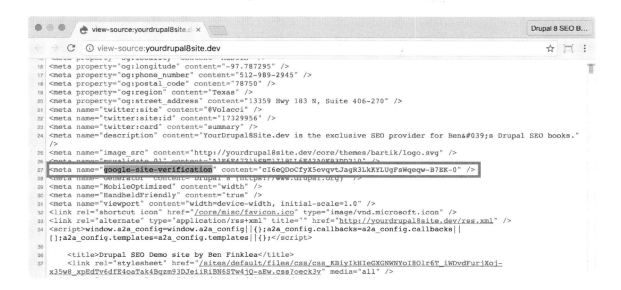

13. Go to the front page of your website. View source and search for `google-site-verification`. You will see the new meta tag as highlighted in the screenshot.

14. Return to **Google Search Console** and click the **Verify** button.

15. You will get a message that says *"Congratulations, you have successfully verified your ownership of http://yourDrupal8site.dev/."*

☐ *Submit XML sitemap to Google*

Now that you've verified your website, you can submit your XML sitemap to Google.

1. Visit **Google Search Console** at https://www.google.com/webmasters/ and sign in.

2. Select your site from the list.

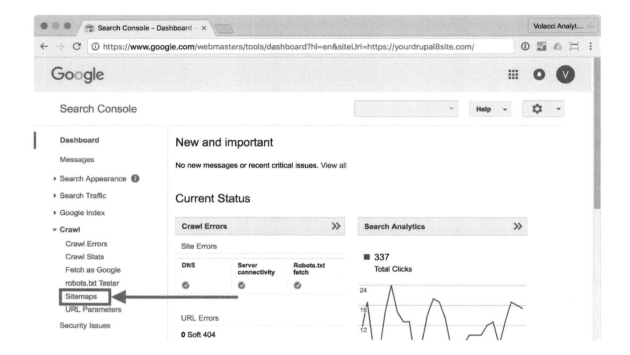

3. Click on **Crawl > Sitemaps** in the left-hand navigation.

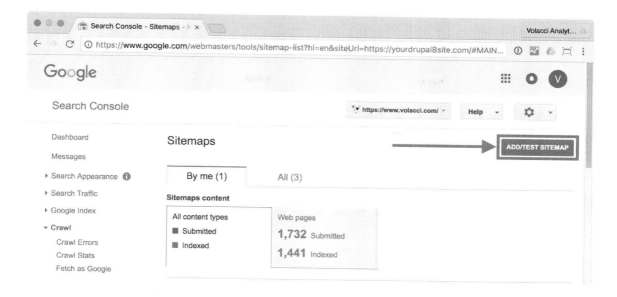

4. Click the **Add/Test Sitemap** button.

5. Enter `sitemap.xml` in the blank provided and click the **Submit** button.

6. You will get a message, *"Item submitted. Refresh the page."*

7. Refresh the page to verify your sitemap has been submitted.

That's it! You've submitted your XML sitemap to Google. It may take a few days for Google to retrieve it and even longer before they index the pages. You can track their progress in **Google Search Console > Crawl > Sitemaps**.

Now, let's submit the same XML sitemap to Bing.

Submit Your Site to Bing

☐ *Get a Microsoft Account*

Microsoft's Bing search engine runs a distant second to Google. Still, it provides over 10% of search volume on the web and shouldn't be ignored.

There's significant value in the tools that Bing provides to webmasters. At a minimum, you'll use it to submit your XML sitemap.

If you don't already have one, you can sign up for free at

https://signup.live.com/newuser.aspx

☐ *Authenticate with Bing Webmaster Tools & submit your XML sitemap*

By authenticating your website, you prove to Microsoft that you own that domain. Then, Microsoft will accept your XML sitemap and start sending you alerts if there are any issues with your site.

> *Note: This process varies slightly depending on if you've already submitted a site to Bing before. The keys are: submit your site, paste the code into your site, and verify it with Bing.*

1. Visit **Bing Webmaster Tools** at https://www.bing.com/webmaster/home/ and sign in with your Live ID.

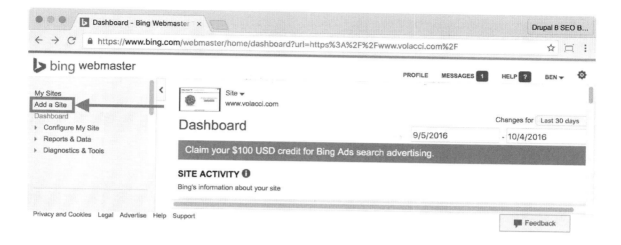

2. Click the "Add a Site" link in the left side.

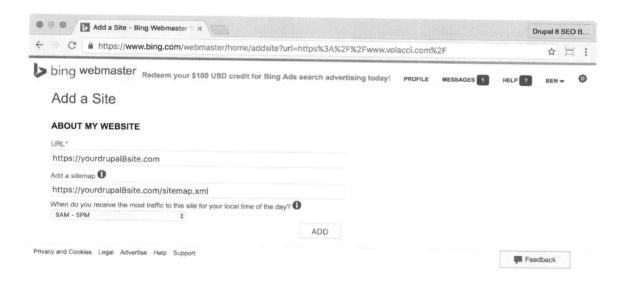

3. Fill out the form on the following page with your contact information, making sure to enter your XML sitemap's URL (usually https://yourDrupal8site.com/sitemap.xml) in the **Add a sitemap** field.

4. Click the **ADD** button.

5. On the next page, under **Option 2: Copy and paste a <meta> tag in your default webpage**, copy just the content part of the meta tag from the

page. It will look something like this:

A1F6F47215SBT1I19LL6F42A0K93DD210

6. On your Drupal 8 site, go to **Manage > Configuration > Search and metadata > Metatag** (Coffee: "metatag") or visit `http://yourDrupal8site.dev/admin/config/search/metatag` in your browser.

7. Click on the **Edit** button next to **Front Page**.

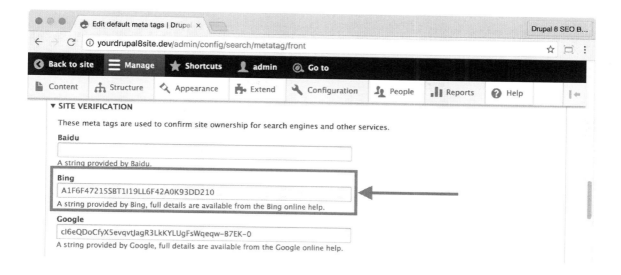

8. Under **Site Verification > Bing**, paste in the verification meta tag that you copied from Bing Webmaster Tools.

9. Click the **Save** button at the bottom of the page.

10. Go to **Manage > Configuration > Development > Performance** (Coffee: "performance") or visit

    http://yourDrupal8site.dev/admin/config/development/performance in your browser.

11. Click the **Clear all caches** button.

12. Go to the front page of your website.

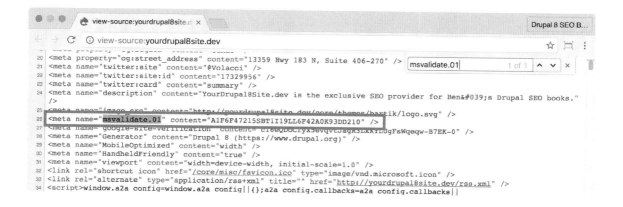

13. View source and search for "msvalidate". You will find the new meta tag.

14. Now return to **Bing Webmaster Tools** and click the **Verify** button.

15. After a few seconds, you will see the **Bing Webmaster** dashboard with your newly-added website listed.

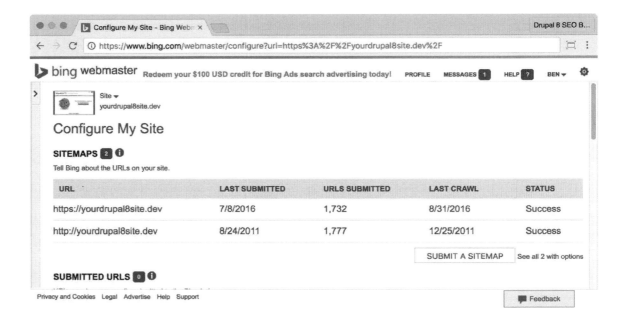

16. In the left-hand navigation menu, click **Configure My Site** and ensure your XML sitemap is listed. It may show a status of "*Pending*" for a while after you submit it.

Now that you've submitted to the top two search engines, let's make sure other search engines can find your XML sitemap, too.

☐ Add the XML Sitemap to Your `robots.txt` File

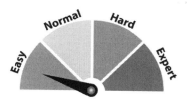

> **SEO Training Camp**
> *http://www.sitemaps.org/protocol.html#submit_robots*

About adding the XML Sitemap to your robots.txt file

Any search engine can use the XML sitemap but submitting it to every search engine would be a tedious process. Fortunately, there is a standard for communicating your XML sitemap location: the `robots.txt` file.

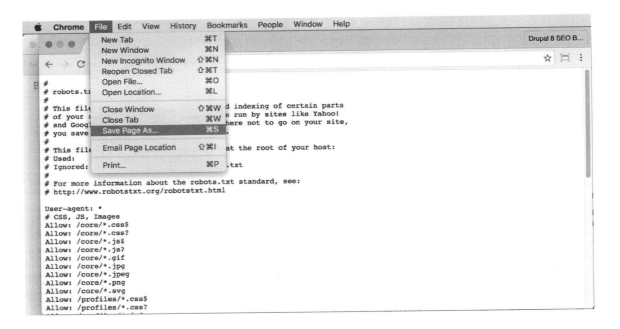

1. Download your **robots.txt** file. Point your browser to `https://yourDrupal8site.dev/robots.txt` and select "Save" from the browser's file menu.

2. Using a text editor like Notepad or TextEdit, open your robots.txt file.

3. Danger! Avoid complex word processing programs as they add invisible markup that makes the file unusable by crawlers.

4. Add this line to the bottom of your **robots.txt** file:

`sitemap: https://yourDrupal8site.dev/sitemap.xml`

and save the file. (If you are not using an SSH certificate, use

`sitemap: http://yourDrupal8site.dev/sitemap.xml`)

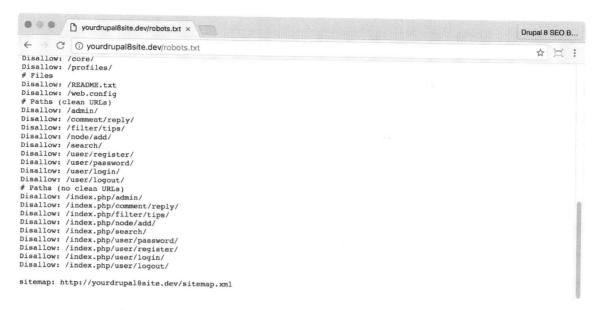

```
yourdrupal8site.dev/robots.txt ×                              Drupal 8 SEO B...

← → C  ⓘ yourdrupal8site.dev/robots.txt                    ☆ ⊐ ⋮

Disallow: /core/
Disallow: /profiles/
# Files
Disallow: /README.txt
Disallow: /web.config
# Paths (clean URLs)
Disallow: /admin/
Disallow: /comment/reply/
Disallow: /filter/tips/
Disallow: /node/add/
Disallow: /search/
Disallow: /user/register/
Disallow: /user/password/
Disallow: /user/login/
Disallow: /user/logout/
# Paths (no clean URLs)
Disallow: /index.php/admin/
Disallow: /index.php/comment/reply/
Disallow: /index.php/filter/tips/
Disallow: /index.php/node/add/
Disallow: /index.php/search/
Disallow: /index.php/user/password/
Disallow: /index.php/user/register/
Disallow: /index.php/user/login/
Disallow: /index.php/user/logout/

sitemap: http://yourdrupal8site.dev/sitemap.xml
```

5. Upload the file back to the root level of your Drupal site, replacing your existing robots.txt file. For me, the root level is **/var/www/drupalvm/drupal/web** but your installation will likely vary. If you don't have FTP access, ask your developer or hosting company to help you.

6. Verify that you did it properly by visiting https://yourDrupal8site.dev/robots.txt and refreshing the page.

That's it! Now, any other search engines can find the location of your XML sitemap by visiting your **robots.txt** file.

The Google Analytics Module

https://www.drupal.org/project/google_analytics

Credits & Thanks

Thank you to hass for his untiring effort to maintain this module and port it to Drupal 8. Thank you Mike Carter (budda on Drupal.org) for creating the *Google Analytics* module.

> **SEO Training Camp**
> - **https://dev.acquia.com/blog/drupal-8-module-of-the-week/drupal-8-module-of-the-week-google-analytics/05/07/2016/15806**
> - **https://www.google.com/analytics/**

About the Google Analytics Module

The *Google Analytics* module adds the **Google Analytics code snippet** to your website and allows you to control how and when it is used.

Google Analytics is a valuable tool for any web marketer. It allows you to find valuable insights about your visitors including demographics, behavior on your site, where they found you online, what keywords they used to find you, and more.

However, Google Analytics isn't perfect. For example, it tracks all visitors by default—even Admins. The *Google Analytics* module can be configured to show the Google

Analytics code snippet only when a non-admin is visiting the site. This keeps your data clean and your reports more useful.

> *Tip: Google Tag Manager is an alternative way to install Google Analytics and it's how we do it on our more advanced client websites. It's more flexible than Google Analytics alone but it adds a layer of complexity that you may not want. Although I don't go into it in this book, you can read about how to install Google Analytics using Google Tag Manager here:*
> *https://www.volacci.com/blog/installing-google-tag-manager-and-universal-analytics-your-drupal-website*

☐ *Install and Enable the Google Analytics Module*

1. Install the **Google Analytics** module on your server. (See Chapter 1 for more instructions on installing modules.)

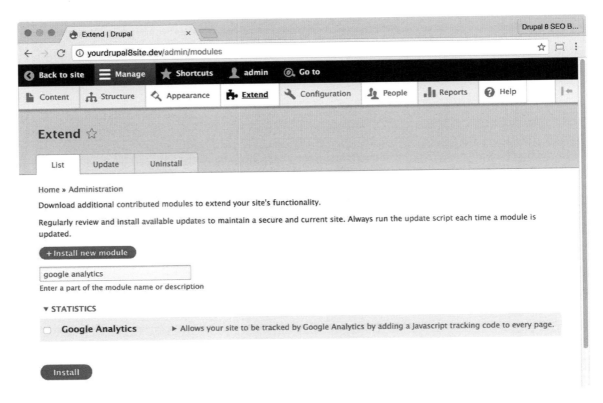

2. Go to the Extend page: Click **Manage > Extend** (Coffee: "extend") or visit `http://yourDrupal8site.dev/admin/modules`.

3. Select the checkbox next to "Google Analytics" and click the **Install** button at the bottom of the page.

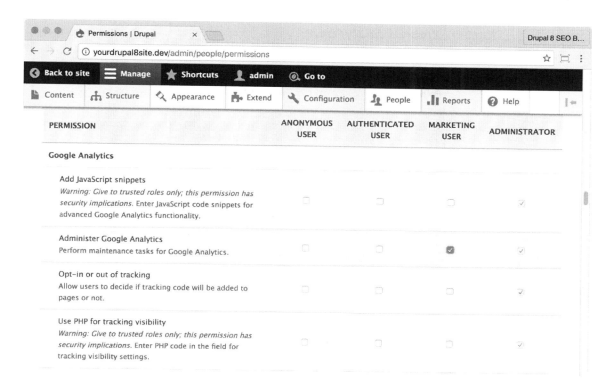

If necessary, give yourself permissions to use the *Google Analytics* module.

1. Click **Manage > People > Permissions** (Coffee: "perm") or visit
    `http://yourDrupal8site.dev/admin/people/permissions`.

2. Select the appropriate checkbox for "Administer Google Analytics".

> *Note: There are three more permissions for Google Analytics module that you probably won't use.*

3. Click the **Save permissions** button at the bottom of the page.

☐ *Configure the Google Analytics module*

First, you'll create a Google Analytics property for your website. Then, you'll add the tracking code to the *Google Analytics* module in Drupal 8.

1. Sign in to **Google Analytics** at
https://www.google.com/analytics/. Use your existing Google ID or the
one you created earlier in this chapter.

2. ☐ Create a Google Analytics **property** for your website.

3. First-time Google Analytics users will need to **Sign up**, agree to the terms
of service, and create an account. As part of the process, you'll create your first
Google Analytics property.

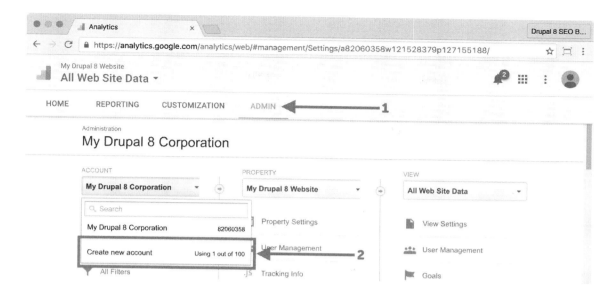

4. If you already have a Google Analytics account, click the **Admin** link. From the left hand **ACCOUNT** column, click the Accounts drop-down menu and select **Create new account**.

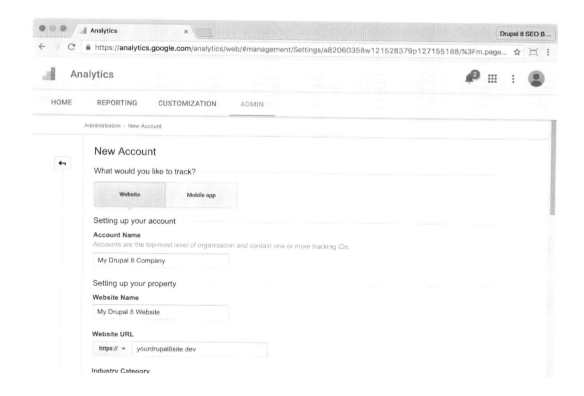

5. Fill out the New Account form and click the **Get Tracking ID** button at the bottom of the page.

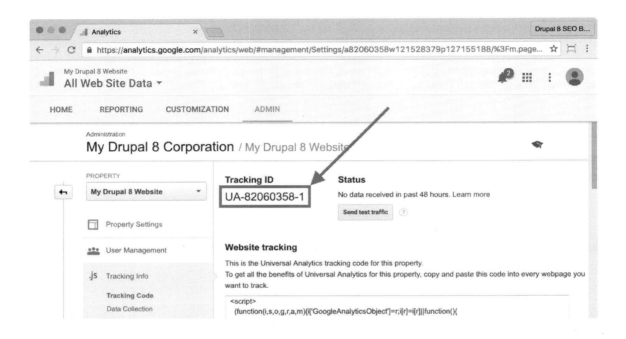

6. The tracking ID for your website will be on the next page. Copy it.

7. On your Drupal 8 site, click **Manage > Configuration > System > Google Analytics** (Coffee: "google") or visit `http://yourDrupal8site.dev/admin/config/system/google-analytics` in your browser.

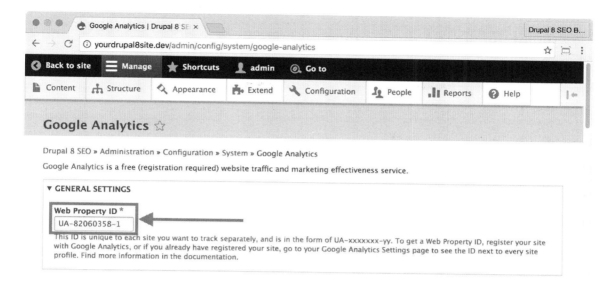

8. Under **General Settings > Web Property ID**, paste in the Google Analytics Tracking ID copied from the Google Analytics website.

9. Click the **Roles** tab and select the *Anonymous user* checkbox. You may want to track more roles depending on your website configuration.

10. The rest of the *Google Analytics* module settings should be left on default for most sites.

11. Click the **Save configuration** button at the bottom of the page.

☐ *Verify the Google Analytics installation*

1. Open an incognito window in your browser. Go to your website's homepage and view source.

2. Look for your Google Analytics Tracking ID number to verify that the Google Analytics code is installed on your website.

3. Open your website in an Incognito window. Click around on your site to generate some test traffic.

4. Now, log in to Google Analytics and go to your property.

Status

Receiving traffic in past 48 hours.

1 active users right now (including 1 from test traffic). See details in real-time traffic reports.

Test traffic sent.

5. Click **Admin > Property > .js Tracking Info > Tracking Code**.

6. At the top, under "Status", you should see "Receiving traffic…".

☐ *Cache the Google Analytics code for faster performance*

Now that you have Google Analytics installed on your website, you will start to see data collect in your Google Analytics account. Once you start to see data, take one more step to make things perform a little faster:

1. On your Drupal site, click **Manage > Configuration > System > Google Analytics** (Coffee: "google") or visit `http://yourDrupal8site.dev/admin/config/system/google-analytics` in your browser.

2. Open the Advanced Settings drop-down near the bottom of the page.

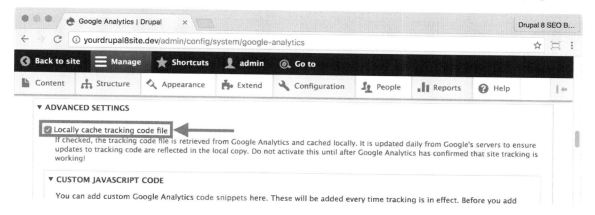

3. Select the checkbox next to **Locally cache tracking code file**.

4. Click the **Save configuration** button at the bottom of the page.

SEO Training Camp
You can learn about how to get the most from Google Analytics here: https://analyticsacademy.withgoogle.com/

Conclusion

In this chapter we covered fifteen *SEO Checklist* items by installing and configuring:

- the ***XML Sitemap*** module and
- the ***Google Analytics*** module.
- You **submitted your XML sitemap** to Google and Bing,
- You **placed a link to the XML Sitemap in your robots.txt file** to help other search engines find it, and
- You **installed Google Analytics** to track information about your visitors and make better decisions about your future marketing.

By completing these items, Google and Bing are crawling the pages of your website for you. Rest assured that your site is fully represented in the major search engines. Thanks to Google Analytics, you can now see what visitors are doing on your site. It's a huge and important step to making Drupal 8 as effective as it can be and helping you make great marketing decisions.

In the next chapter, we'll continue down the *SEO Checklist* with a look at **Breadcrumbs** and **Schema.org**.

Chapter 6:
Optimizing Content, Part 1

"Feel the rhythm! Feel the rhyme! Get on up, it's bobsled time!"

Sanka Coffie

COOL RUNNINGS

Items Covered

- Easy Breadcrumbs module
- RDF UI module
- Linkit module
- D8 Editor Advanced link module

YOU PERFORM YOUR BEST WHEN you're not worried about the little things that could go wrong. Whether you're getting organized around the office or piloting an Olympic bobsled, if you're comfortable then your performance will improve.

Let's make your content comfortable! This chapter will guide you through:

- adding signposts at the top of your site in the form of *breadcrumbs*,
- adding *RDF markup* to your content that will help the search engines understand it better, and
- creating valid, aliased and marked up links throughout your content.

Get on up, it's SEO markup time!

The Easy Breadcrumbs Module

https://www.drupal.org/project/easy_breadcrumb

Credits & Thanks

Thank you to Roger Padilla (sonemonu on Drupal.org) for creating this module.

Thank you to these contributors: Ashish Thakur (ashhishhh), Greg Boggs, and Rakesh James (rakesh.gectcr).

> *SEO Training Camp*
> *https://developers.google.com/search/docs/data-*
> *types/breadcrumbs*

About the Easy Breadcrumbs module

The *Easy Breadcrumbs* module uses the current URL (path alias) and the current node title to automatically create breadcrumbs.

Breadcrumbs are those essential navigational elements that show visitors where they are on a website. They look something like this:

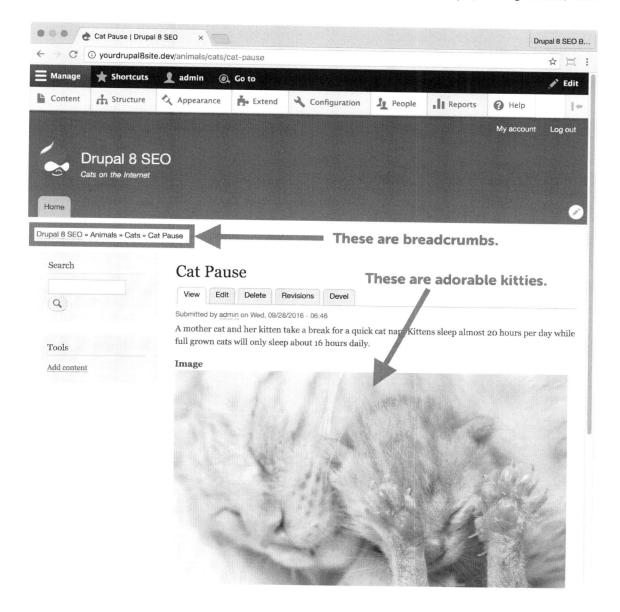

Breadcrumbs help your SEO by revealing the hierarchy in your content. Google loves hierarchy because it helps them understand your content. Visitors love hierarchy, too, because it helps them figure out your site's organizational structure.

☐ *Install and Enable the Easy Breadcrumbs Module*

1. Install the *Easy Breadcrumbs* module on your server. (See Chapter 1 for more instructions on installing modules.)

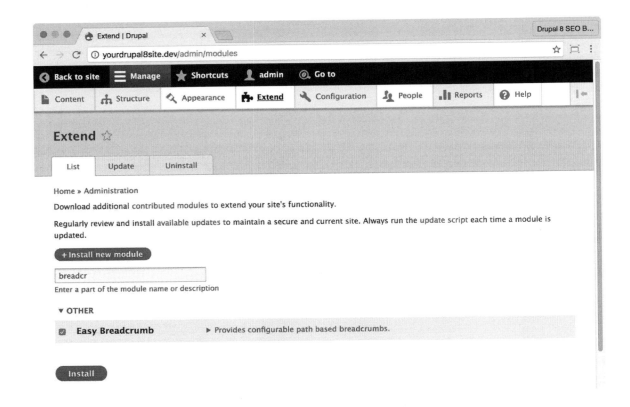

2. Go to the Extend page: Click **Manage > Extend** (Coffee: "extend") or visit `http://yourDrupal8site.dev/admin/modules` in your browser.

3. Select the checkbox next to "Easy Breadcrumbs" and click the **Install** button at the bottom of the page.

There are no separate permissions required for the *Easy Breadcrumbs* module.

☐ Configure the Easy Breadcrumbs module

1. Click **Configuration** > **User Interface** > **Easy Breadcrumbs** (Coffee: "breadcrumbs") or visit `http://yourDrupal8site.dev/admin/config/user-interface/easy-breadcrumb` in your browser.

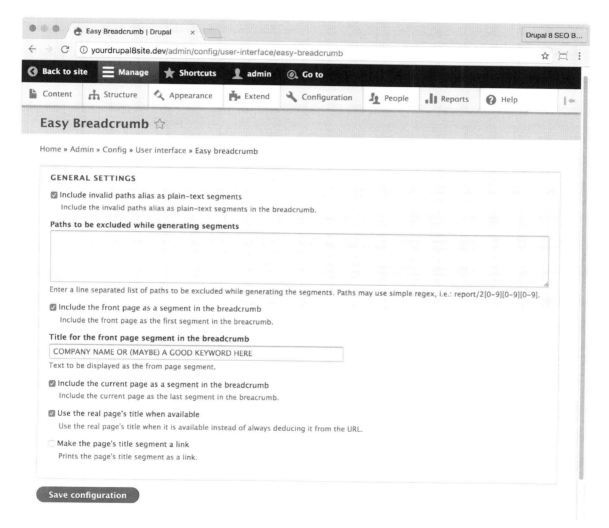

2. Configure the module as demonstrated in the screenshot above:

    a. Select the checkbox next to "Include invalid paths alias as plain-text segments".

> *Warning: An invalid path doesn't resolve. You should probably show the site hierarchy in your breadcrumbs even if you haven't built it yet as it's helpful to visitors. Then, go back through your site and make sure that each breadcrumb link resolves to an existing page.*

    b. Select the checkbox next to "Include the front page as a segment in the breadcrumb".

    c. For the "Title for the front page segment…" field, use something more descriptive than "Home". You could use your company name or experiment with using a keyword that describes your website, service, or product.

    d. Select the checkbox next to "Include the current page as a segment in the breadcrumb". This gets your title on the page again which is useful for keyword optimization.

    e. Select the checkbox next to "Use the real page's title when available", which will use the page title instead of the URL for the last (right-most) breadcrumb.

3. Click the **Save configuration** button at the bottom of the page.

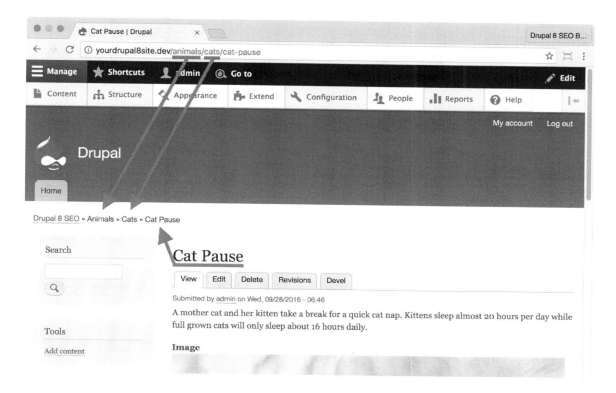

Easy Breadcrumb module builds the breadcrumbs from the path. Each / becomes a part of the breadcrumb. The first breadcrumb comes from the Easy Breadcrumb configuration page while the title of the node becomes the last breadcrumb.

Schema.org and the RDF Module

As you have seen in the section on meta tags, it is beneficial to describe your content in search-engine-friendly ways. A second, more robust standard than meta tags for marking up your content is **Schema.org**.

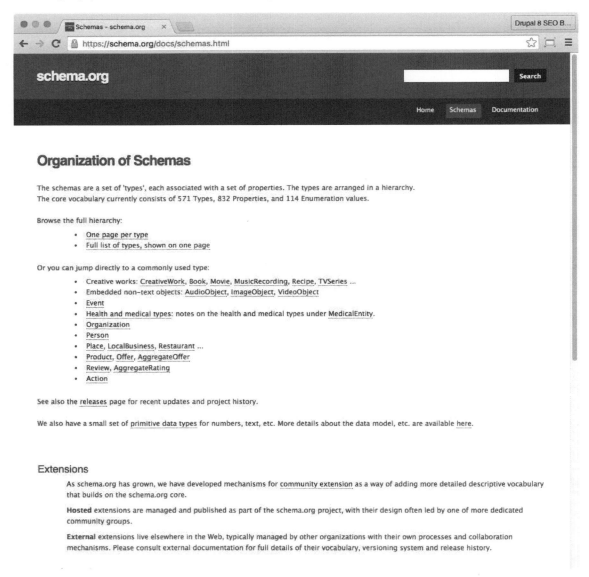

Schema.org

The Schema.org website describes the Schema.org project as "...a joint effort, in the spirit of sitemaps.org, to improve the web by creating a structured data markup schema supported by major search engines. On-page markup helps search engines understand the information on web pages and provide richer search results."

Schema.org markup functions similarly to meta tags except instead of being at the top of the page; schema.org markup is placed directly on each bit of content that it is describing. Google can understand your content correctly because you were explicit about what it means.

Is that number near the product the price or the discount? Is that date when the content posted or the birthdate of the person on the page? Is that the title of the movie, the title of the event, or the name of the event venue? Schema.org clears up these questions and countless others.

You can implement Schema.org on your website using *Resource Description Framework*, or *RDF* for short. It's a family of *World Wide Web Consortium (W3C)* specifications designed as a metadata model. W3C developed RDF as a way to markup content to describe it better.

> **Note: There is another way of adding markup like this to your website called JSON-LD. But, at the time of this writing, there isn't a good module to implement it for Drupal 8 yet.**

Drupal RDF module

Handily, Drupal 8 has RDF built in. There's a Core module called "RDF" that is probably already enabled (but you can check to be sure at http://yourDrupal8site.dev/admin/modules).

RDF isn't meant to be touched much. In fact, Drupal 8 doesn't provide any mechanism for setting RDF tags to you, the marketer. To add Schema.org markup to your content, you need the *RDF UI* module.

The RDF UI Module

https://www.drupal.org/project/rdfui

> **Warning: As of this writing, you should use the development release of the RDF UI module dated 2016-Aug-21 or later. When beta 2 or later comes out, you should try it on a development server before using on a live site (as with all modules.)**

Credits & Thanks

Thank you to Sachini Herath (Sachini on Drupal.org) for creating this module.

Thank you to Stéphane Corlosquet (scor) who created the excellent predecessor module that got rolled into Drupal Core. Kudos!

> **SEO Training Camp**
> * **https://schema.org/**
> * **https://www.youtube.com/watch?v=l31MlxOCG-4**

About the RDF UI module

The *RDF UI* module allows site builders to integrate Schema.org seamlessly during or after the site building process on Drupal 8.

☐ *Install and Enable the RDF UI Module*

1. Install the *RDF UI* module on your server. (See Chapter 1 for more instructions on installing modules.)

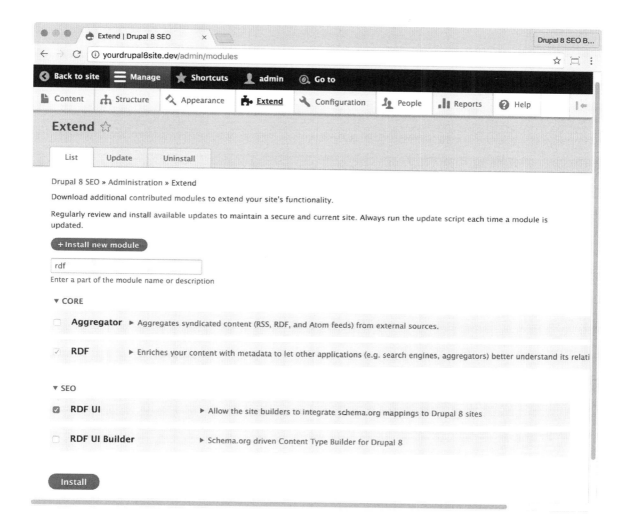

2. Go to the Extend page: Click **Manage > Extend** (Coffee: "extend") or visit `http://yourDrupal8site.dev/admin/modules` in your browser.

3. Select the checkbox next to "RDF UI" and click the **Install** button at the bottom of the page.

4. There are no separate permissions required for the *RDF UI* module.

☐ Set Schema.org schemas for your content

To configure Schema.org settings, you need to go to the setup page for each of your Content Types. We'll start with Blog Postings.

1. Go to **Manage > Structure > Content Types > Blog Postings** (or whatever you have named your blog post content type).

    5. Select the vertical tab near the bottom of the page called **Schema.org Mappings**.

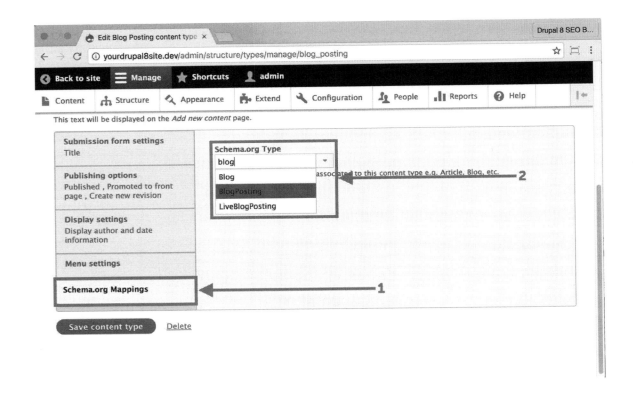

6. In the field **Schema.org type**, start typing "Blog…" and then select "BlogPosting" from the type-ahead menu.

7. Click the **Save content type** button at the bottom of the page.

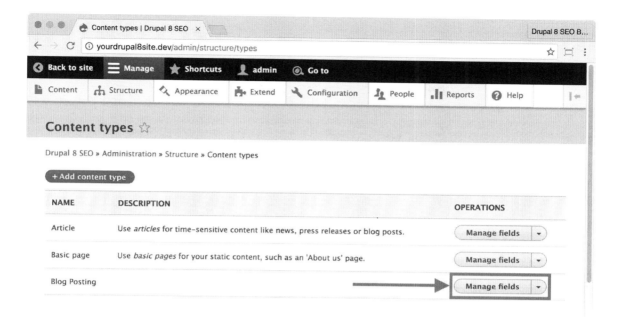

8. Now go to **Admin > Structures > Content types**
(http://yourDrupal8site.dev/admin/structure/types) and click the
Manage Fields button next to "Blog Postings".

9. Click the **RDF Mappings** sub-tab.

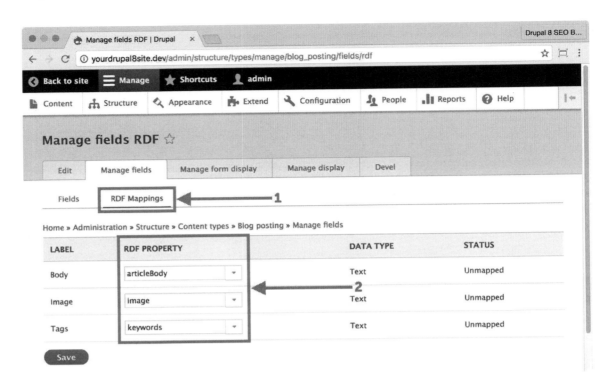

10. Select the **RDF Property** for each field listed and click the **Save** button. (See below for links to different schemas.)*

11. Repeat steps 1-7 for each of your Content Types.

*Full list of schemas: https://schema.org/docs/schemas.html

Some common Schema.org schemas:

      Article - https://schema.org/Article

      Blog Posting - https://schema.org/BlogPosting

      Event - https://schema.org/Event

      Person - https://schema.org/Person

      Product - https://schema.org/Product

Here's the kind of markup that the RDF module adds to the page after you've used *RDF UI* to assign Schema.org properties to it:

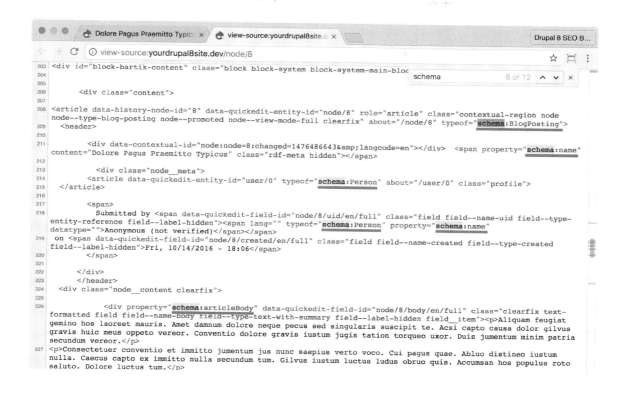

The Linkit Module

https://www.drupal.org/project/linkit

Credits & Thanks

Thank you to Emil Stjerneman (anon on Drupal.org) for creating and maintaining this module. Thanks Didrik Nordström (betamos) for your contributions.

About the Linkit module

The *Linkit* module provides an autocomplete field in your WYSIWYG content editor for linking to other pages on your site. It gives your content creators an easy way to create links, and it ensures that links added to your content are well formed, up to date, and automatically use the proper path.

Properly formed and placed links are a powerful strategy for any SEO campaign. The *Linkit* module is an excellent tool to help a good link strategy.

☐ Install and Enable the Linkit Module

1. Install the *Linkit* module on your server. (See Chapter 1 for more instructions on installing modules.)

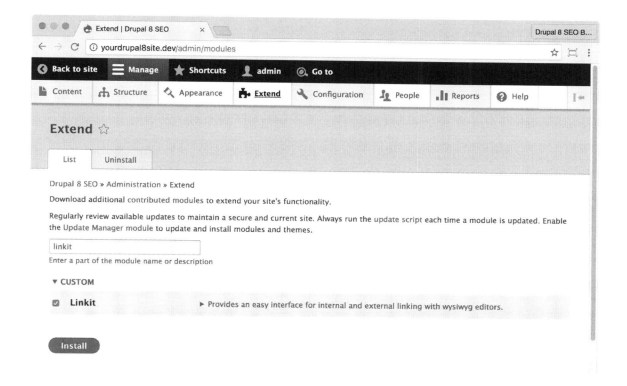

2. Go to the Extend page: Click **Manage > Extend** (Coffee: "extend") or visit `http://yourDrupal8site.dev/admin/modules` in your browser.

3. Select the checkbox next to "Linkit" and click the **Install** button at the bottom of the page.

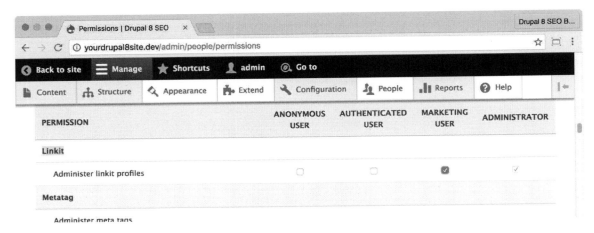

If necessary, give yourself permissions to use the *Linkit* module.

1. Click **Manage > People > Permissions** (Coffee: "perm") or visit
http://yourDrupal8site.dev/admin/people/permissions.

2. Select the appropriate checkbox for "Administer linkit profiles".

3. Click the **Save permissions** button at the bottom of the page.

☐ *Configure the Linkit module*

To use the *Linkit* module, you need to enable it, select the profile, add it as a filter, arrange the filters in the proper order, and a couple of other settings. Please follow these steps carefully:

1. Visit the *Linkit* admin page at
http://yourDrupal8site.dev/admin/config/content/linkit (Coffee:
"linkit").

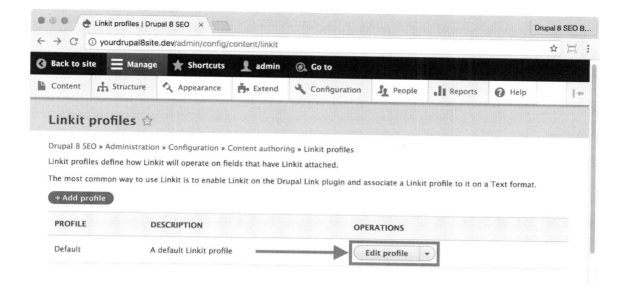

2. Click the "Edit profile" link next to the Default profile.

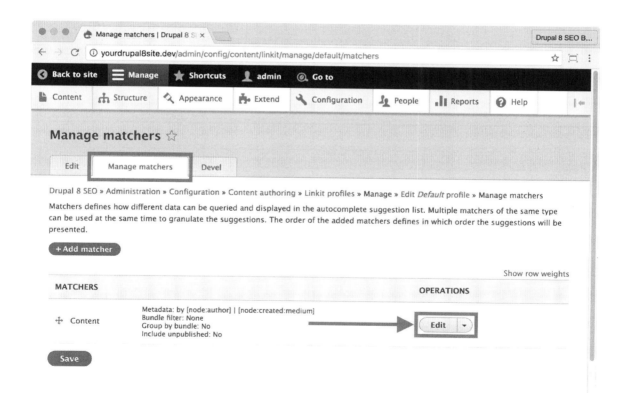

3. Click the "Manage matchers" tab. Then, click the **Edit** button next to the Content matcher.

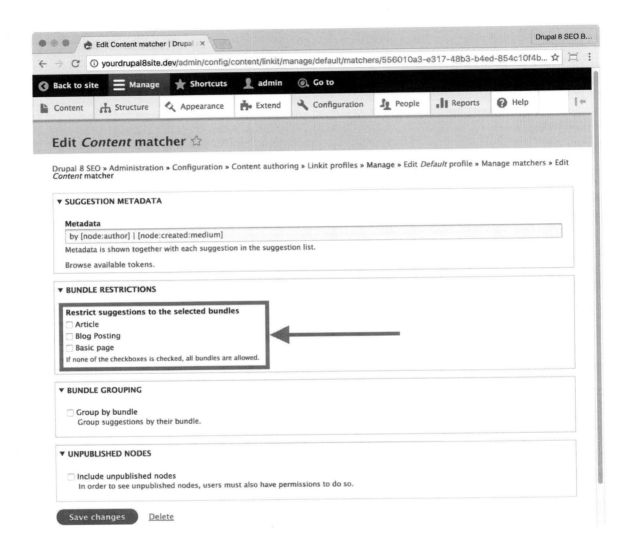

4. Here, you can select which types of content will show up in the link selector. Leave all of the checkboxes unchecked to include all content types.

5. You can also allow links to unpublished Nodes. Be careful, though, that you're not linking to content that Google or your visitors cannot see.

6. If you made any changes, click the **Save changes** button at the bottom of the page.

☐ *Configure Text Formats to use the Linkit module.*

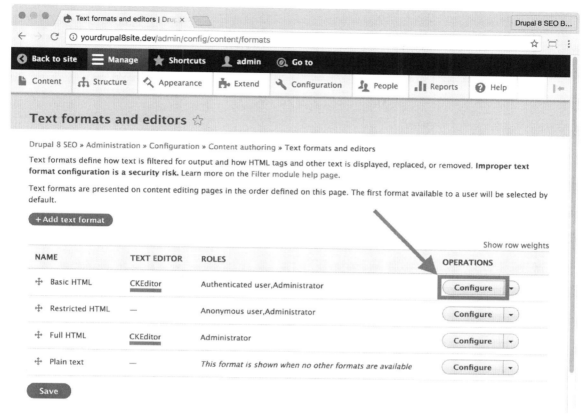

1. Go to the **Manage > Configuration > Content Authoring > Text Formats and Editors** (Coffee: "text") or visit

http://yourDrupal8site.dev/admin/config/content/formats in your browser.

2. Note which text formats use the CKEditor. (CKEditor is the default WYSIWYG editor in Drupal). Click the **Configure** button next to the first one.

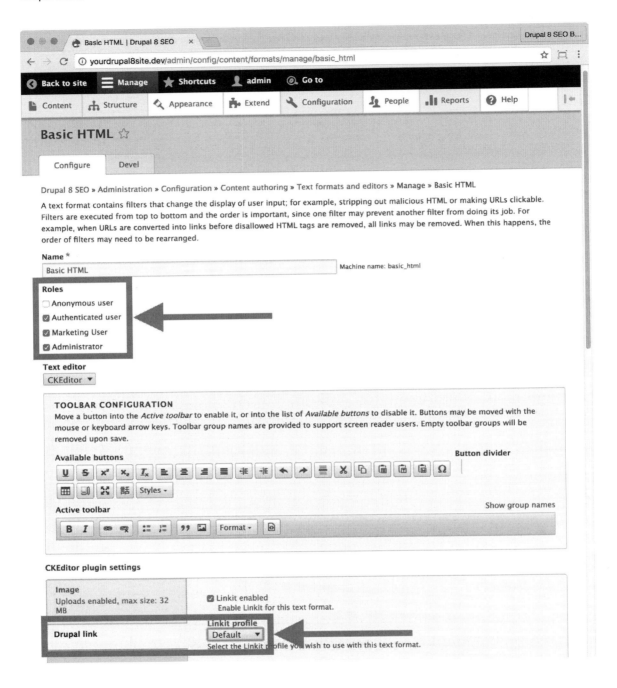

3. Next to "Roles", assign the roles that can use the Linkit module.

4. Scroll down the page to see the "CKEditor plugin settings" set of vertical tabs. Click on the **Drupal link** tab.

Tip: There are two sets of vertical tabs on this page so scroll down carefully or search the page for "Drupal link" to find it.

5. Select the checkbox next to "Linkit enabled". The "Linkit profile" field will appear. For the "Linkit profile" field, select "Default".

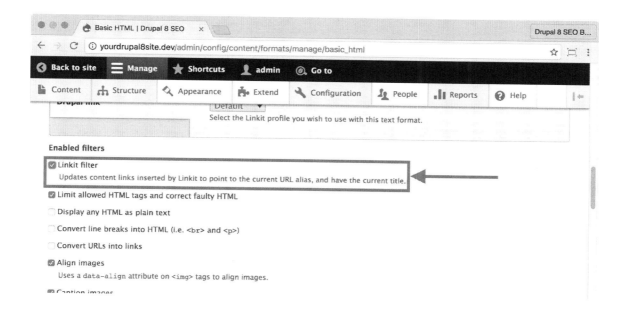

6. Scroll down a little more and select the checkbox next to "Linkit filter" under "Enabled filters".

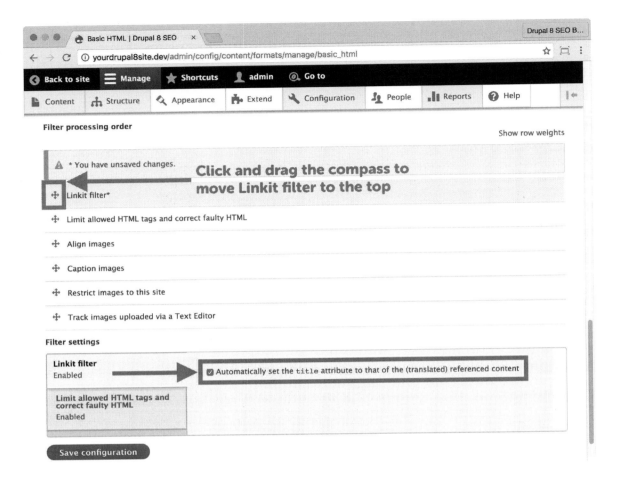

7. Scroll down to "Filter processing order". Drag "Linkit filter" to the top of the list.

8. Under **Filter settings > Linkit filter**, make sure the checkbox next to "Automatically set the title attribute to that of the (translated) referenced content" is checked. This setting will put an SEO-friendly "title" element on the link.

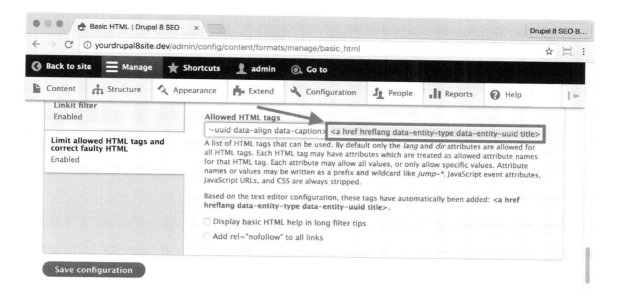

If the "Limit allowed HTML tags and correct faulty HTML" tab is not there, then skip step 10. Don't worry; it's not necessary for all text types.

9. Under "Limit allowed HTML tags and correct faulty HTML" you will see a field called "Allowed HTML tags". Put your cursor in this field and use the arrow keys on your keyboard to scroll to the right until you find the link element <a href...>. Make sure that "title" is part of the <a href…> element. If not, add title to the element. It will look something like this: "<a href hreflang data-entity-type data-entity-uuid **title**>". (bold added)

10. Click the **Save configuration** button at the bottom of the page.

11. Repeat steps 3-10 for each of the Text formats that use the CKeditor. These steps will probably work if you're using a text editor other than CKeditor, too. Always click the **Save configuration** button after each one.

Using the Linkit module to add links to your nodes

The *Linkit* module replaces the built-in linking mechanism in your WYSIWYG editor. As you can see below, select text in the node you're editing and click the **link** button.

1. Open a node and click the "Edit" tab or create a new node.

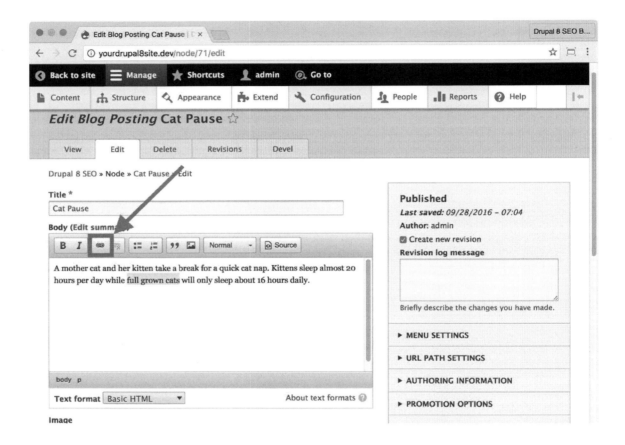

2. Select some text that you wish to link. Click the **link** button.

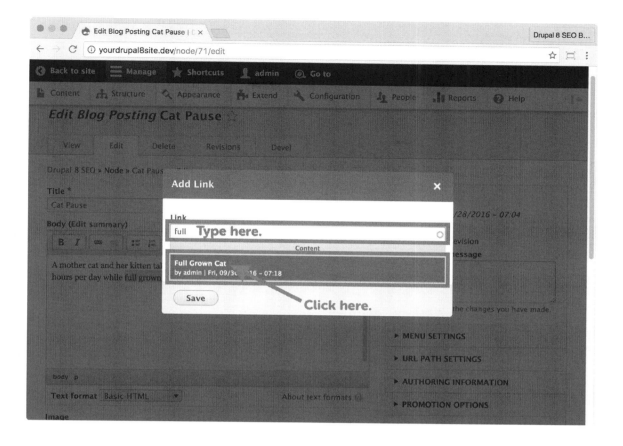

3. In the modal window that opens, start typing the name of a node that you are linking to. As you type, a list of matching nodes will appear. Select the node that you want to link to.

4. The text that is displayed as the link will show up as something like: "entity:node/102". This is an internal Drupal link and will always resolve to the node path—which is an SEO-friendly, keyword-rich link. Click the **Save** button.

5. Your newly added link will appear as blue and underlined. Scroll to the bottom of the page and click the **Save and keep published** button (or **Save and publish** if it's a new node.)

6. View the source HTML of the node you just edited and find your link. You'll see that it is using the proper, SEO-friendly path and it has used the title of the node that you linked to as the link title.

While it can prove tedious to configure the first time, *Linkit* module provides useful functionality for your website's content creators.

The D8 Editor Advanced Link Module

https://www.drupal.org/project/editor_advanced_link

Credits & Thanks

Thank you to Edouard Cunibil (DuaelFr on Drupal.org) for creating and maintaining this module.

SEO Training Camp
https://moz.com/learn/seo/title-tag

About the D8 Editor Advanced Link Module

The *D8 Editor Advanced link* module allows you to define `title`, `class`, `id`, `target`, and `rel` for links in CKEditor. This functionality helps your SEO by placing more text information about each link on the page.

☐ *Install and Enable the D8 Editor Advanced Link Module*

1. Install the *D8 Editor Advanced link* module on your server. (See Chapter 1 for more instructions on installing modules.)

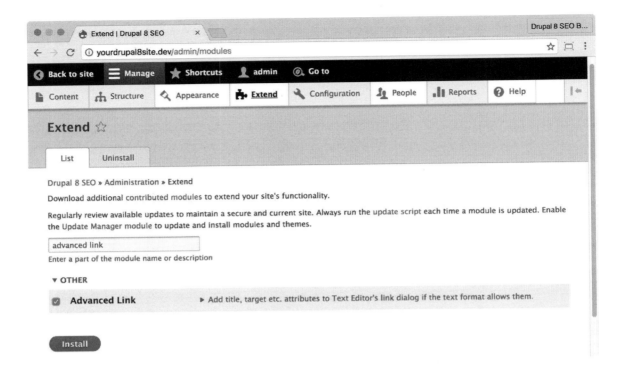

2. Go to the Extend page: Click **Manage > Extend** (Coffee: "extend") or visit `http://yourDrupal8site.dev/admin/modules` in your browser.

3. Select the checkbox next to **Advanced Link** and click the **Install** button at the bottom of the page.

There are no separate permissions required for the *D8 Editor Advanced link* module.

□ *Configure text formats to use D8 Editor Advanced link module*

1. Go to the **Manage > Configuration > Content Authoring > Text Formats and Editors** (Coffee: "text") or visit `http://yourDrupal8site.dev/admin/config/content/formats` in your browser.

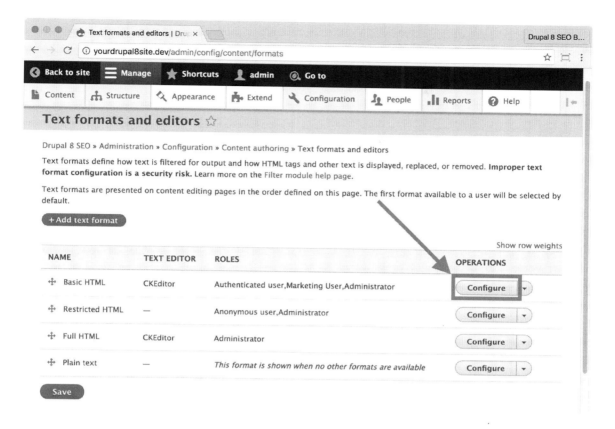

2. Click the **Configure** button next to the first text type listed. This will allow you to edit the configuration options.

3. Scroll down to the vertical tab near the bottom of the page called **Limit allowed HTML tags and correct faulty HTML**. If that tab is not there, then skip to step 6.

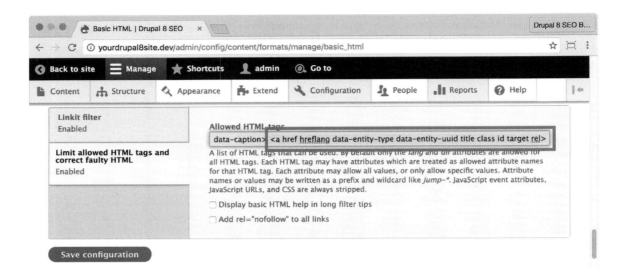

4. Under the **Limit allowed HTML tags and correct faulty HTML** you will see a field called "Allowed HTML tags". Put your cursor in this field and use the arrow keys on your keyboard to scroll to the right until you find the link element <a href...>. Add "title class id target rel" to the link element. It will look something like this but could vary: "<a href hreflang data-entity-type data-entity-uuid **title class id target rel**>". (bold added)

> *Tip: You can include the CSS tags "class" and "id" if you need them.*

5. Click the **Save configuration** at the bottom of the page.

6. Repeat steps 1-5 for each of the text formats. Always click the **Save configuration** button after each one.

Using the D8 Editor Advanced link module when adding links to your nodes

1. Open a node and click the **Edit** tab or create a new node.

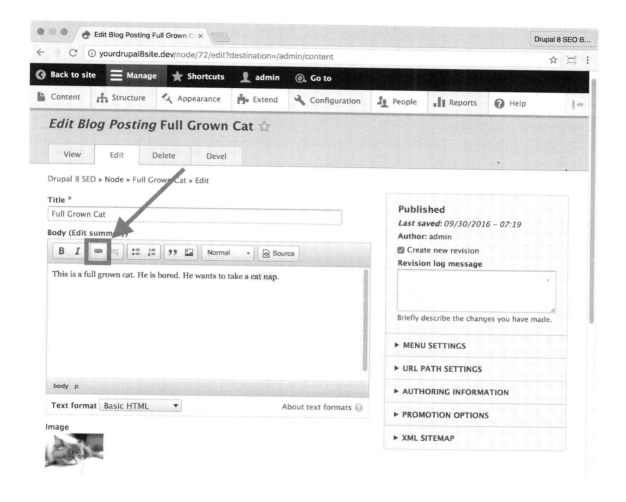

2. Select the text to be linked. Click the link image button in the editor menu bar.

3. Open the **Advanced** drop-down.

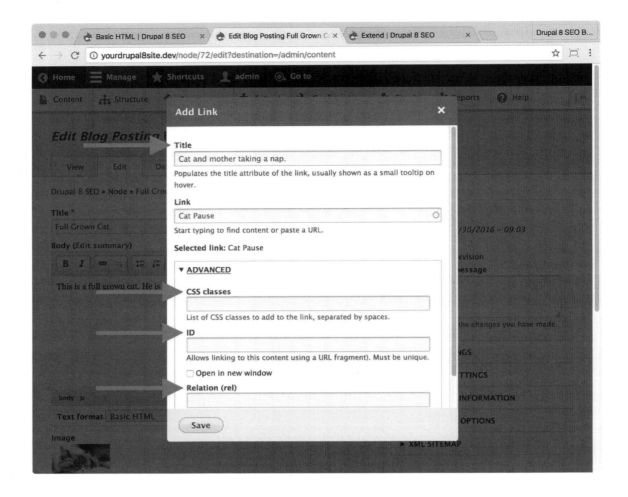

4. There are options to add a **Title** and **Rel,** and a checkbox that will open the link in a new window. Fill in appropriate fields as needed.

5. Click the **Save and keep published** button (or **Save and publish** if it's a new node.)

Conclusion

In this chapter we covered nine *SEO Checklist* items:

- You created navigational elements on your nodes with the ***Easy Breadcrumbs*** module,
- You gave yourself access to RDF with the ***RDF UI*** module,
- You marked up your node content with **Schema.org** settings,
- You avoided the nightmare of broken links with the ***Linkit*** module, and
- You added key fields to your links with the ***D8 Editor Advanced link*** module.

By completing these items, you content is much more optimized for Google and SEO than it was before.

In the next chapter, we'll continue down the *SEO Checklist* with a look at the ***W3C Validator*** module and the ***Sitemap*** module.

Chapter 7:
Optimizing Content, Part 2

"Being perfect is about being able to look your friend in the eye and know that you didn't let them down because you told them the truth. And that truth is you did everything you could."

Coach Gaines
FRIDAY NIGHT LIGHTS

Items Covered

- W3C Validator module
- Sitemap module
- Search 404 module

Players win games, but teams win championships. Yes, a superstar player can lead a breakaway, make the shot, or catch the long ball for the last minute touchdown. However, individual success doesn't happen without a great supporting cast of players that can bring out their best.

In this chapter, we're going to cover some of the bit players in your Drupal 8 SEO journey. The supporting cast that helps your superstar content shine: validating your website's code, putting together a sitemap for your visitors, and making sure that they can find your content even when they're lost. These may be minor players, but they're valuable members of the team, nevertheless.

The W3C Validator Module

https://www.drupal.org/project/w3c_validator

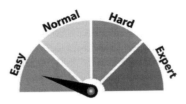

Credits & Thanks

Thank you to Pedro Lozano (Pedro Lozano on Drupal.org) for creating this module.

Big thanks to Dominique CLAUSE (Dom.) who maintains it currently and created the Drupal 8 version that we use today.

About the W3C Validator module

The *W3C Validator* module provides a Drupal interface to use the *W3C Markup Validator*.

The World Wide Web Consortium (W3C) is an international community where Member organizations, a full-time staff, and the public work together to develop Web standards. Led by Web inventor Tim Berners-Lee and CEO Jeffrey Jaffe, W3C's mission is to lead the Web to its full potential. One of the ways they fulfill this mission is the *W3C Validator* which checks the markup validity of Web documents in HTML, XHTML, and more.

The *W3C Validator* module uses W3C standards to tell you if your web pages are properly formed or if there are issues to fix. This HTML and CSS checker helps your SEO because badly-written pages might confuse the Google bot or even your visitors' browser. Perfection is not necessary, though. Many websites have problems with their HTML and still rank in Google. It's better to be safe than sorry.

☐ Install and Enable the W3C Validator Module

1. Install the **W3C Validator** module on your server. (See Chapter 1 for more instructions on installing modules.)

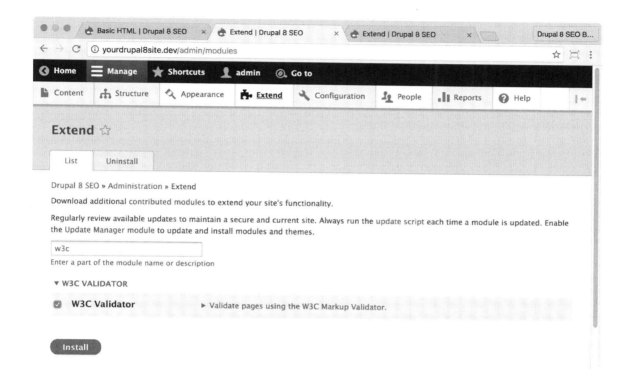

2. Go to the Extend page: Click **Manage > Extend** (Coffee: "extend") or visit `http://yourDrupal8site.dev/admin/modules` in your browser.

3. Select the checkbox next to "W3C Validator" and click the **Install** button at the bottom of the page.

There are no separate permissions required for the *W3C Validator* module.

> *Note: As of this writing, I needed to use the dev version of the W3C Validator module.*

☐ *Configure the W3C Validator module*

1. Click **Manage > Reports > W3C Validation Report** (Coffee: "w3c") or visit `http://yourDrupal8site.dev/admin/reports/w3c_validator` in your browser.

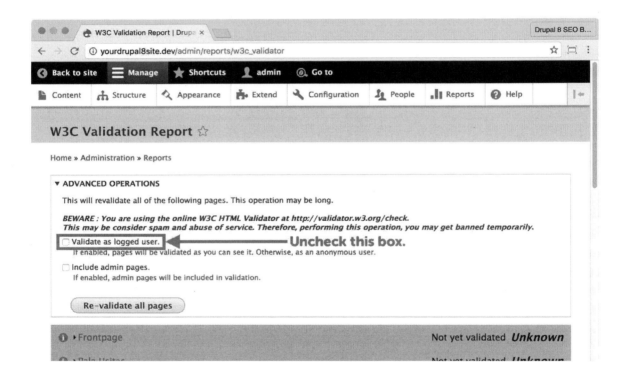

2. Configure the module as shown above:

   a. Uncheck "Validate as logged user." Google visits your website as an anonymous visitor, so that's what you should validate.

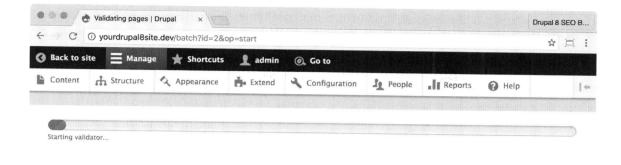

3. Click the **Re-validate all pages'** button. You will be asked if you're sure. Click the **Confirm** button.

> *Tip: Validation may take some time for large websites. Stay on the page until the validator finishes.*

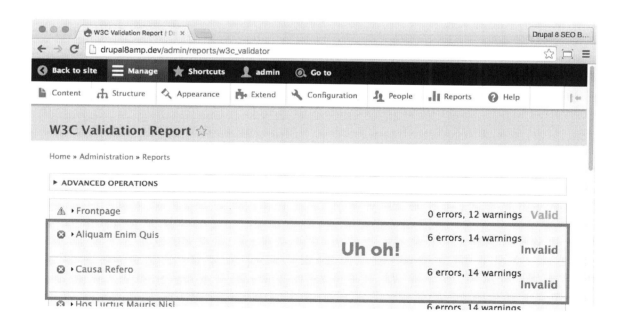

4. The next page shows you the warning and errors that the validator has returned on each page.

5. Click the drop down arrow next to a page to see the specific errors for that page.

You can turn these errors and warnings over to your developer or themer. W3C validator is strict while Googlebot is much more forgiving. In other words, fix the big problems and knock out as many as your budget allows without obsessing over every single error.

The Sitemap Module

https://www.drupal.org/project/sitemap

Credits & Thanks

Thank you to Anna Kalata (akalata) who has done a great job of porting this module to Drupal 8. Thank you to killes@www.drop.org (killes@www.drop.org on Drupal.org) who created this module.

About the Sitemap module

The *Sitemap* module provides an *HTML sitemap* that gives visitors an overview of your website. It also displays RSS feeds for blogs and categories.

The *Sitemap* module makes it easier for visitors to find content and that improves SEO. This helpful page increases visitor *time on site* and reduces *bounce rate*.

Search engines will also crawl the HTML sitemap which, along with the XML sitemap, increases positive exposure for your content.

☐ *Install and Enable the Sitemap Module*

1. Install the *Sitemap* module on your server. (See Chapter 1 for more instructions on installing modules.)

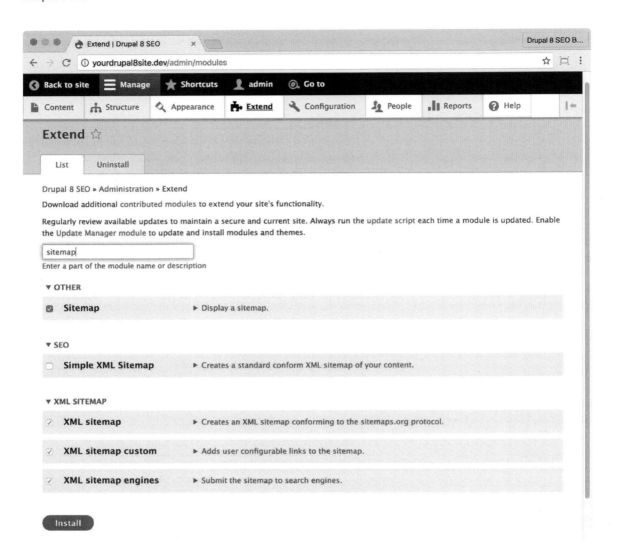

2. Go to the Extend page: Click **Manage > Extend** (Coffee: "extend") or visit `http://yourDrupal8site.dev/admin/modules` in your browser.

3. Select the checkbox next to "Sitemap" and click the **Install** button at the bottom of the page.

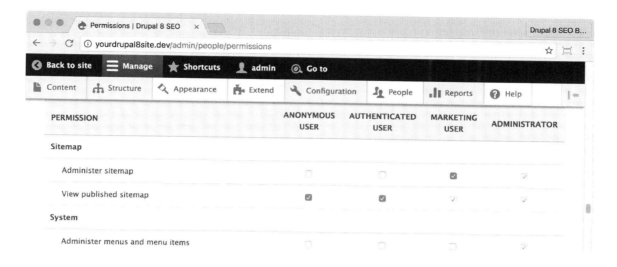

Configure permissions for the Sitemap module.

1. Click **Manage > People > Permissions** (Coffee: "perm") or visit `http://yourDrupal8site.dev/admin/people/permissions`.

2. Select the appropriate checkbox to give yourself permissions for "Administer sitemap".

3. Since you want visitors to view the sitemap, you'll need to select the checkboxes to allow **Anonymous User** and **Authenticated User** to "View published sitemap".

4. Click the **Save permissions** button at the bottom of the page.

☐ Configure the Sitemap module

1. Click **Manage > Configuration > Search and metadata > Sitemap** (Coffee: "sitemap") or visit `http://yourDrupal8site.dev/admin/config/search/sitemap` in your browser.

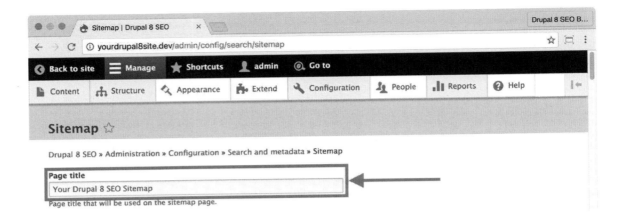

2. Set the **Page title** using some keywords or your site name.

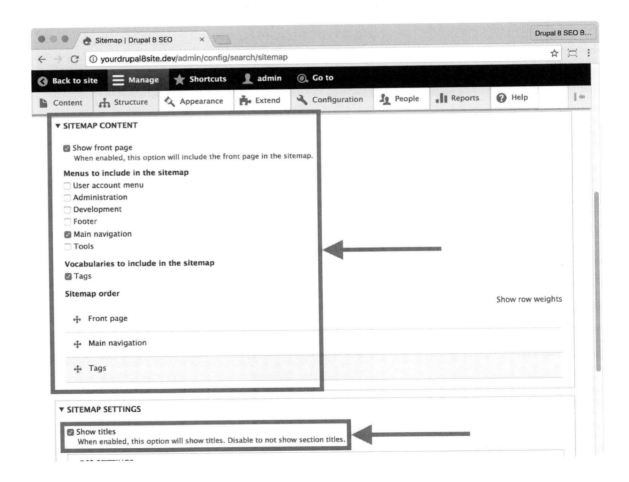

3. Select the appropriate checkboxes under **Menus to include in the Sitemap**. Likely your **Main navigation** or any other visitor-facing menus.

4. Under **Vocabularies to include in the sitemap**, select your main categories and **Tags** if you have them.

5. Under **Sitemap Settings**, select the "Show titles" checkbox.

6. Click the **Save configuration** button at the bottom of the page.

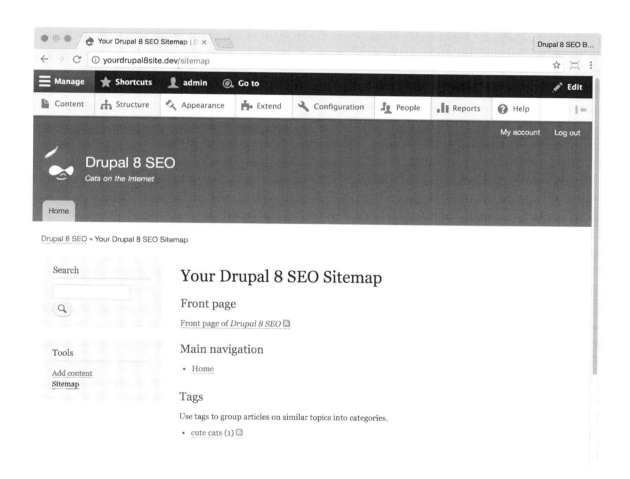

You can view the sitemap at http://yourDrupal8site.dev/sitemap.

The little orange icons next to each section are links to RSS feeds. Visitors who want to subscribe to your site and return when you've published new content will use that link in their newsreader applications.

The Search 404 Module

https://www.drupal.org/project/search404

Credits & Thanks

Thank you to larssg (larssg on Drupal.org) for creating this module and thanks to zyxware for their support in maintaining it.

About the Search 404 Module

When a website visitor goes to a URL that doesn't exist, the *Search 404* module shows them alternative pages that might contain the content they are seeking. The module performs a search using the keywords in the missing URL to select appropriate content to show to the lost visitor.

For example, if a visitor goes to http://yourDrupal8site.dev/animals/cute-cats (which I assume doesn't exist on your website) and finds nothing then this module will search for "animals cute cats" and display those search results below the "404 Page Not Found" error.

This tweak to the 404 page helps your SEO by making sure that old or badly written links to your site will still resolve. It helps visitors find your content. You want visitors to find the great content on your site. You especially want Google to be able to find related content if the indexed page has been removed.

☐ *Install and Enable the Search 404 Module*

1. Install the *Search 404* module on your server. (See Chapter 1 for more instructions on installing modules.)

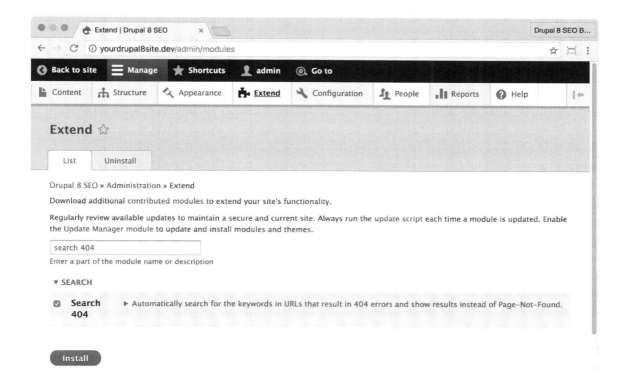

2. Go to the Extend page: Click **Manage > Extend** (Coffee: "extend") or visit `http://yourDrupal8site.dev/admin/modules` in your browser.

3. Select the checkbox next to "Search 404" and click the **Install** button at the bottom of the page.

There are no separate permissions required for the *Search 404* module.

☐ Configure the Search 404 module

1. Go to the **Search 404** module admin page by clicking **Manage > Configuration > Search and metadata > Search 404 Settings** (Coffee: "search404") or visit

`http://yourDrupal8site.dev/admin/config/search/search404` in your browser.

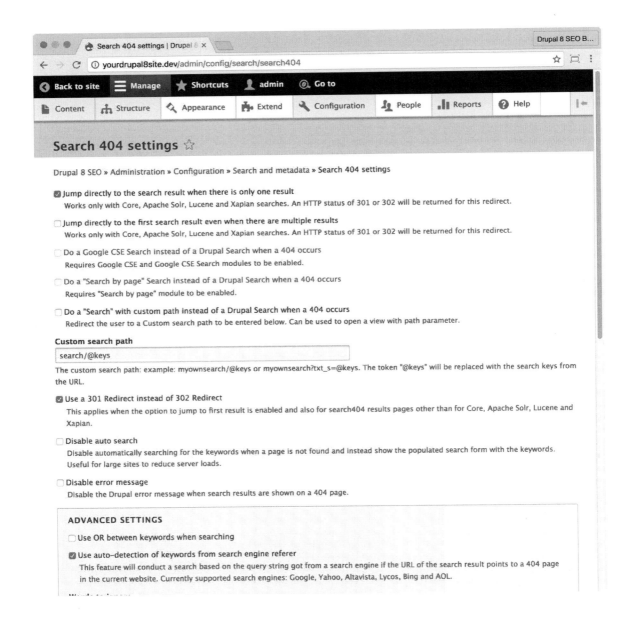

2. Configure the module as shown above:

    A. Select the checkbox "Jump directly to the search result when there is only one result".

    B. Select the checkbox "Use a 301 Redirect instead of 302 Redirect".

    C. Select the checkbox "Use auto-detection of keywords from search engine referer".

    D. Although there are many options on this page, you can leave most of them as you find them.

3. Click the **Save configuration** button.

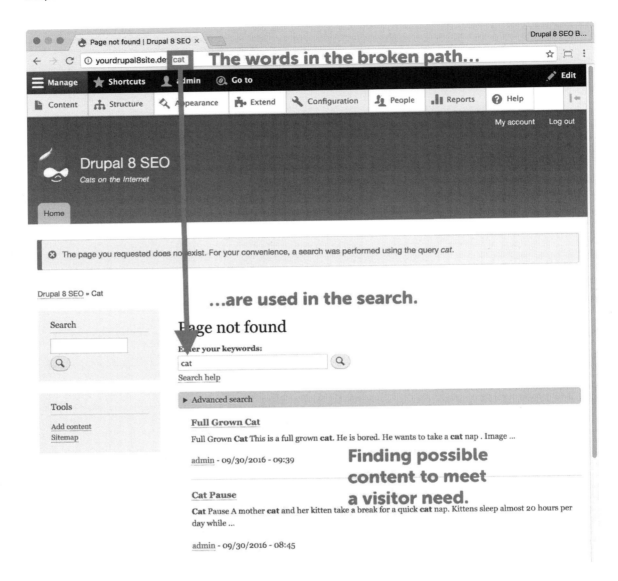

Now, try visiting a page on your site that you know does not exist, like
http://yourDrupal8site.dev/animals/cute-cats. You will see "Page not found" with the
results of a search underneath it.

Conclusion

In this chapter we covered six *SEO Checklist* items:

- You validated your website's HTML with the **W3C Validator** module,
- You made it easier for visitors to find and follow your content with the **Sitemap** module, and
- You helped "lost" visitors to find the right content with the **Search 404** module.

Your content is now well optimized. Along with the tasks you completed in the previous chapter, you know that visitors and Google can find your site, see what's there, get to the content that means the most to them, and engage more than ever before.

In the next chapter, we'll continue down the *SEO Checklist* with a look at the **Yoast SEO** module, **diff** module, and the **Scheduler** module.

Chapter 8: Page Optimization

"The inches we need are everywhere around us. They're in every break of the game, every minute, every second."

Tony D'Amato
Any Given Sunday

Items Covered

- *Yoast SEO* module
- *Diff* module
- *Create New Revision* setting
- *Scheduler* module

FOOTBALL IS A GAME OF INCHES. With surprising frequency, the game comes down to minor gaps in execution. On third down, a halfback stumbles mere inches short of the first down. The field goal attempt glances off the left upright and out of play. An out-of-position cornerback is a half-step behind defending a deep pass and the opposing wide receiver scores. That's a nine-point swing and likely the game.

Like football, search engine optimization is a game of inches: a `title` tag that's missing a keyword, a body that doesn't talk about the topic, metadata that isn't quite right. Together, that's enough to kick you off the front page of Google.

So far we've been optimizing on a site-wide basis—changes to admin settings that affect every page of your site. Now, we dive down into the nitty-gritty, page-by-page stuff that makes up those last few inches. It may get tedious, but in the trenches is where SEO matters most. OMAHA…OMAHA…HUT!!!

The Yoast SEO Module

https://www.drupal.org/project/yoast_seo

Credits & Thanks

Thank you to Bram ten Hove (bramtenhove on Drupal.org) for creating this module. Thank you to these contributors: Kevin Muller (kevinmuller), 7gipsy, and Robert Ragas (RobertRagas). Finally, thanks to GoalGorilla and Lemberg who provided time and resources to this project.

About the Yoast SEO module

The *Yoast SEO* module helps you optimize content around key phrases. It does this by evaluating the text on each node and comparing it to SEO best practices. It will give you a list of suggestions right on the node so you can implement them as you create content. If you don't use the *Yoast SEO* module you must use an outside service (like Moz.com or SearchMetrics) to evaluate your pages which is time consuming.

> *Tip: The Yoast module does a basic evaluation. It's helpful, but you can take your on-page optimizations to the next level using a more advanced tool like Moz. I would do it for your critical content.*

☐ Install and Enable the Yoast SEO Module

1. Install the *Yoast SEO* module on your server. (See Chapter 1 for more instructions on installing modules.)

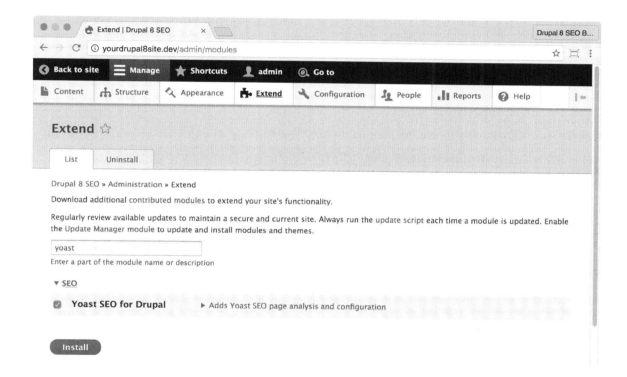

2. Go to the Extend page: Click **Manage > Extend** (Coffee: "extend") or visit `http://yourDrupal8site.dev/admin/modules` in your browser.

3. Select the checkbox next to "Yoast SEO for Drupal" and click the **Install** button at the bottom of the page.

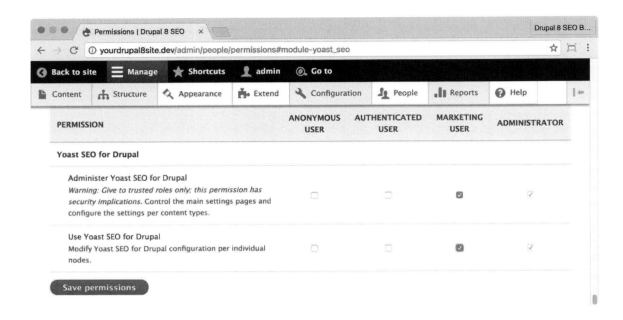

If necessary, give yourself permissions to use the *Yoast SEO* module.

1. Click **Manage > People > Permissions** (Coffee: "perm") or visit
http://yourDrupal8site.dev/admin/people/permissions.

2. Select the appropriate checkboxes for

   • "Administer Yoast SEO for Drupal"

   • "Use Yoast SEO for Drupal"

3. Click the **Save permissions** button at the bottom of the page.

☐ *Configure the Yoast SEO module*

1. Click **Manage > Configuration > Development > Yoast** (Coffee: "yoast")
or visit http://yourDrupal8site.dev/admin/config/yoast_seo in your
browser.

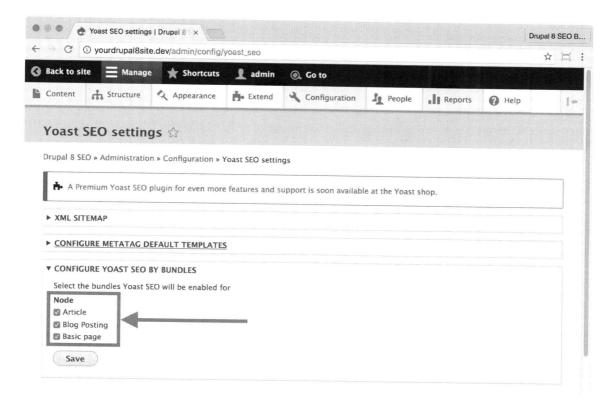

2. Configure the *Yoast SEO* module to work on the appropriate Content Types as shown above.

3. Click the **Save** button.

Using the Yoast SEO module

The *Yoast SEO* module adds functionality to your node edit screens.

1. Create a new blog posting by visiting `http://yourDrupal8site.dev/node/add/blog_posting` in your browser (Coffee: "blog").

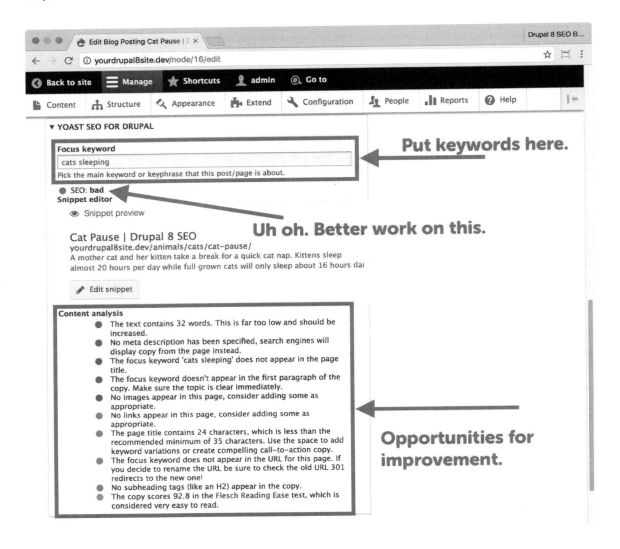

2. Fill out the form to create the new content. As you get down the page, you'll see a drop-down section called **Yoast SEO for Drupal**. Fill in the field **Focus keyword** with your chosen keyword for this page and the *Yoast SEO* module will analyze your content.

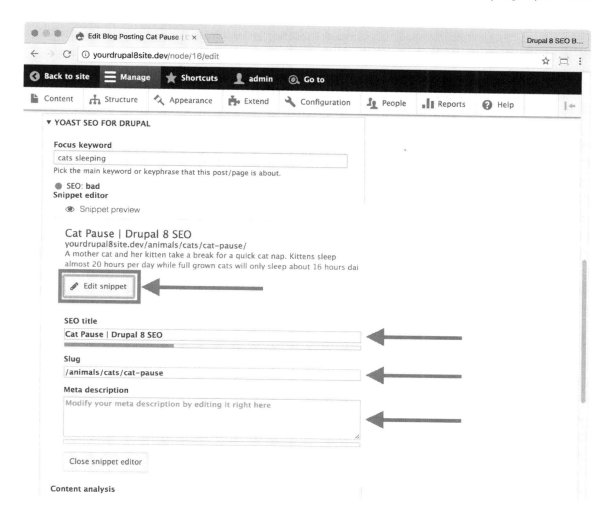

3. The **Snippet editor** shows you what your listing will look like in Google. To fix the Google search snippet, click on each line.

> *Note: Changes here override site-wide settings for this node.*
> *Default settings for other nodes remain unchanged.*

A. Use the "SEO title" field to update your HTML title tag. (Same as going to **Meta tags > Basic tags > Page title** on a node.)

B. Use the "Slug" field to update the URL alias. (Same as **URL Path Settings > URL alias** on a node.)

C. Use the "Meta description" field to update the meta description tag. (Same as going to **Meta tags > Basic tags > Description** on a node.)

4. Fix any issues you find in the **Content Analysis** section of the Yoast SEO section. As you fix those items, the indicator will turn green.

5. Be sure to click the **Save** button at the bottom of the page.

6. Repeat steps 1-5 for every node. Start with the most important ones!

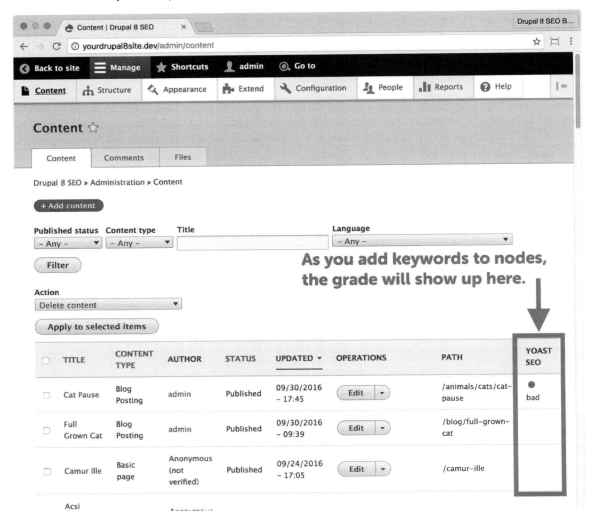

After you add keywords to the **Focus keyword** field on a node, the *Yoast SEO* module will show its score on the **Admin > Content** page.

The Diff Module

https://www.drupal.org/project/diff

Credits & Thanks

Thank you to Moshe Weitzman (moshe weitzman on Drupal.org) for creating the *Diff* module and Brian Gilbert (realityloop) and Lucian Hangea (lhangea) who currently maintain it.

About the Diff module

The *Diff* module shows you differences between revisions to nodes. This function might not sound like a big deal, but if you see an increase or decrease in traffic, it's helpful to see which edits caused the change. If you don't use this module you should keep good records about every little change you make to your site. To reduce the tedious nature of that kind of record keeping, turn on the *Create New Revisions* feature in Drupal Core for each Content Type and use the *Diff* module.

First, we'll turn on Create New Revisions.

☐ *Turn On Create New Revision for All Content Types*

When editing a node, you can create a new revision without overwriting the original. You do this by selecting the **Create new revision** checkbox from the **Publishing options** tab. You can set your Content Types to select the checkbox by default when creating new content. This preset saves a little time and ensures that revisions are saved no matter who edits your content.

1. Click **Manage > Structure > Content types** (Coffee: "content types") or visit http://yourDrupal8site.dev/admin/structure/types in your browser.

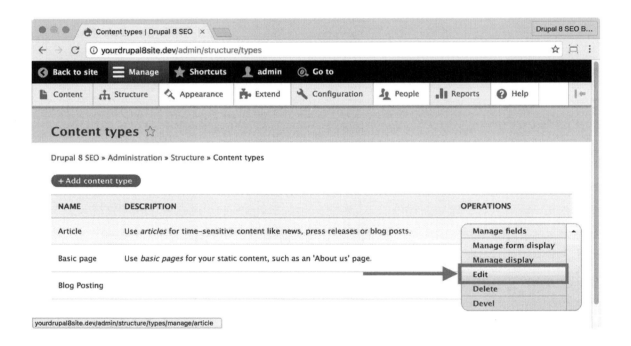

2. Next to your first Content Type, open the drop-down menu next to "Manage fields" and click the **Edit** link.

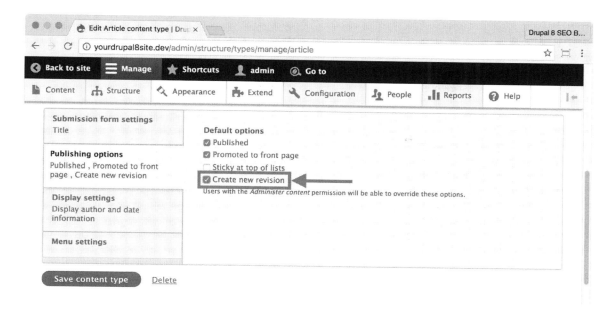

3. Click the **Publishing options** tab and select the **Create new revision** checkbox.

4. Click the **Save content type** button at the bottom of the page.

5. Repeat steps 1-4 for each Content Type.

☐ *Install and Enable the Diff Module*

1. Install the *Diff* module on your server. (See Chapter 1 for more instructions on installing modules.)

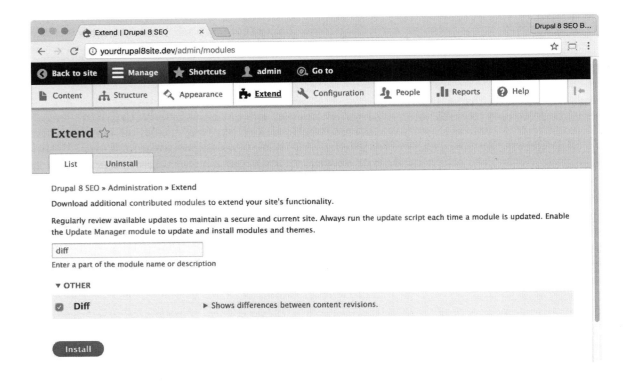

2. Go to the Extend page: Click **Manage > Extend** (Coffee: "extend") or visit `http://yourDrupal8site.dev/admin/modules` in your browser.

3. Select the checkbox next to "Diff" and click "Install" and click the **Install** button at the bottom of the page.

There are no separate permissions required for the *Diff* module.

☐ *Configure the Diff module*

1. Go to the *Diff* admin page by clicking **Manage > Configuration > Content authoring > Diff** (Coffee: "diff") or visit

`http://yourDrupal8site.dev/admin/config/content/diff/general` in your browser.

2.   The default settings on the Settings and Configurable Fields tabs are fine.

> *Note: On the Configurable Fields tab, the Meta tag fields are not trackable with Diff module yet. Hopefully, that is coming soon and you can track this feature here:*
> *https://www.drupal.org/node/2767107.*

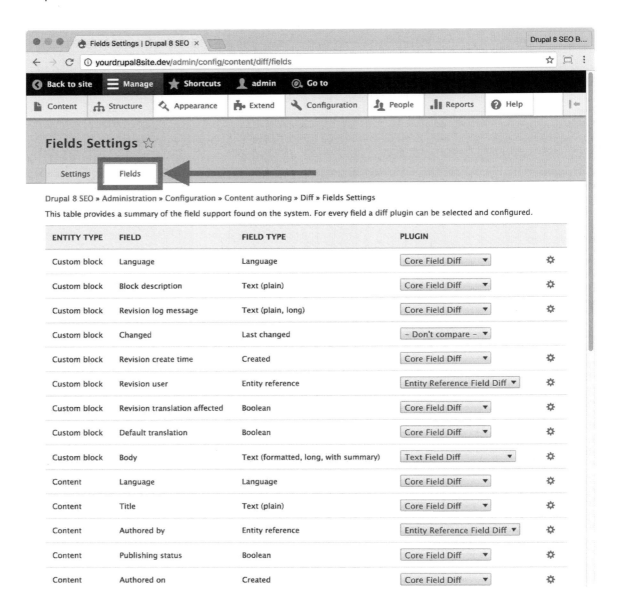

3. Click on the **Fields** tab and ensure the module is configured as shown above, paying close attention to these settings:

    A. **Body** is set to "Text with Summary Field".

    B. **Title** is set to "Core Field Diff".

    C. **Authored by** is set to "Entity Reference Field Diff".

    D. **Revision log message** is set to "Core Field Diff".

4. Click the **Save** button at the bottom of the page.

Using the Diff module

1. Go to a piece of content where you have saved revisions.

2. Click the **Revisions** tab.

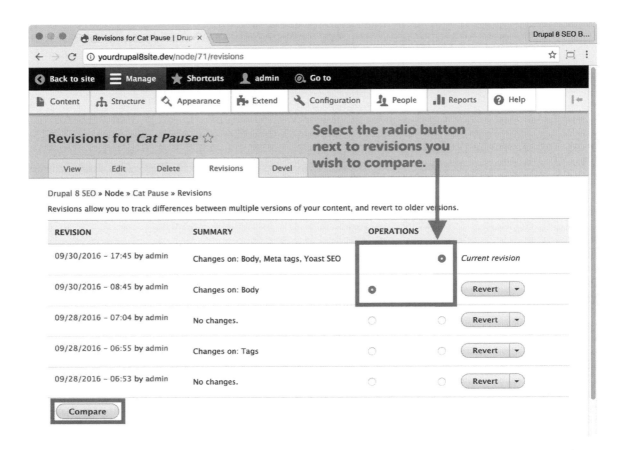

3. You will see a list of revisions with radio buttons. Select the two revisions you wish to compare.

> *Note: If there are no revisions of your node, you will not see this option as there isn't anything to compare.*

4. Click the **Compare** button.

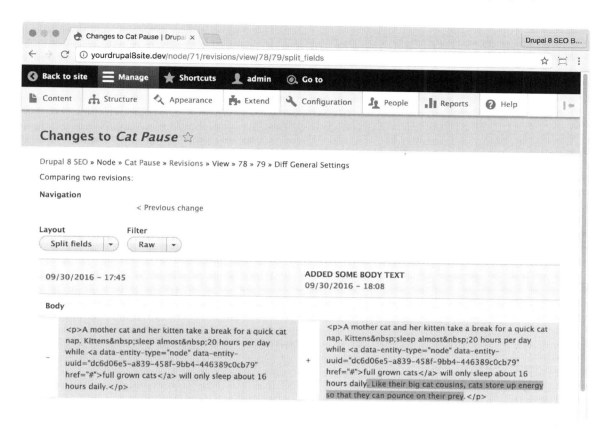

The node's fields are displayed side-by-side with the changes highlighted. This screen makes it easy to see what edits made a difference in your search rankings, click-through rates, and conversions. If you see "+" between the fields, that means some text was added. If you see "-", it means that some text was deleted.

The Scheduler Module

https://www.drupal.org/project/scheduler

Credits & Thanks

Thank you to Moshe Weitzman (moshe weitzman on Drupal.org) for creating this module and Jonathan Smith (jonathan1055) for maintaining it. Thank you to Pieter Frenssen (pfrenssen), Gábor Hojtsy, Eric Schaefer, and Andy Kirkham (AjK) for your contributions.

About the Scheduler module

The *Scheduler* module allows content editors to schedule nodes to be published and unpublished at specified dates and times. This functionality allows you to plan and execute your content strategy which is critical to SEO success.

Let me put it this way: Google loves fresh content. If a website has fresh content, it ranks better. But manually publishing a week's worth of content requires you to remember to post each time you want a new piece of content. The *Scheduler* module allows you to schedule several pieces at once, helping you better manage your time besides helping your SEO.

☐ *Install and Enable the Scheduler Module*

1. Install the *Scheduler* module on your server. (See Chapter 1 for more instructions on installing modules.)

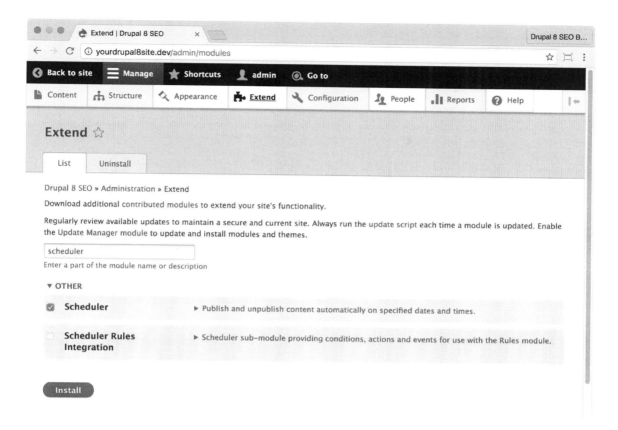

2. Go to the Extend page: Click **Manage > Extend** (Coffee: "extend") or visit `http://yourDrupal8site.dev/admin/modules` in your browser.

3. Select the checkbox next to "Scheduler" and click the **Install** button at the bottom of the page.

4. You may get the message "Some required modules must be enabled" and "You must enable the Actions module…". If you do, click the **Continue** button.

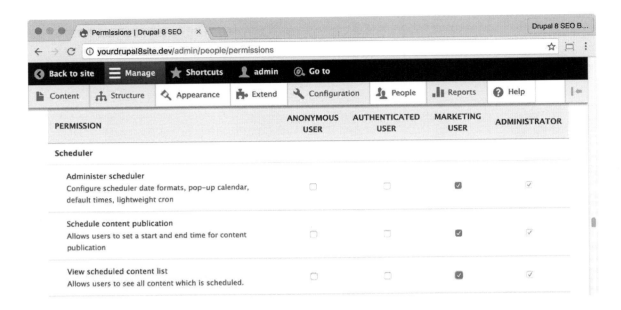

If necessary, give yourself permissions to use the *Scheduler* module.

1. Click **Manage > People > Permissions** (Coffee: "perm") or visit
    `http://yourDrupal8site.dev/admin/people/permissions`.

2. Select the appropriate checkboxes for

    - "Administer scheduler"
    - "Schedule content publication"
    - "View scheduled content list".

3. Click the **Save permissions** button at the bottom of the page.

☐ *Configure the Scheduler module*

1. Go to the *Scheduler* module admin page by clicking **Manage > Configuration > Content authoring > Scheduler** (Coffee: "sch") or visit `http://yourDrupal8site.dev/admin/config/content/scheduler` in your browser.

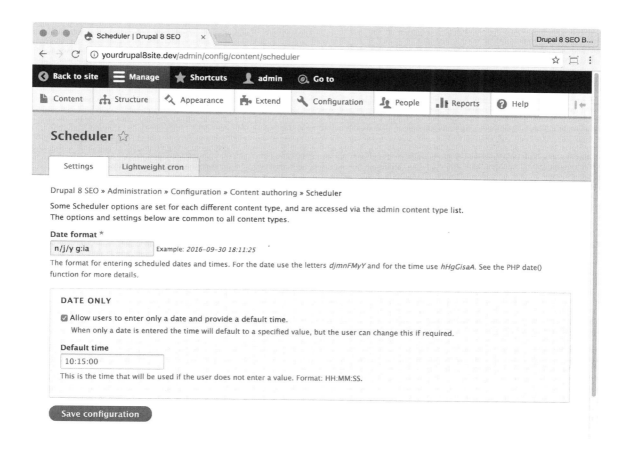

2. Configure the *Scheduler* module:

    A. You can leave the **Date format** setting at the default; however, since I'm from the USA, I prefer to change up the date and time formats. If you're like me then in the **Date format** field, enter "n/j/y g:ia" (without quotes). This setting will give you a formatted date that looks like this: 10/15/16 3:52pm.

> B. Select the checkbox **Allow users to enter only a date and provide a default time**.

> C. Set the **Default time** to 10:15:00. That way, if a time is not specified, it will default to this time, in this case, 10:15 A.M., which is a good time to publish business content.

3. Click the **Save configuration** button.

4. Go to the **Content types** admin page by clicking **Manage > Structure > Content Types** (Coffee: "content types") or visit http://yourDrupal8site.dev/admin/structure/types in your browser.

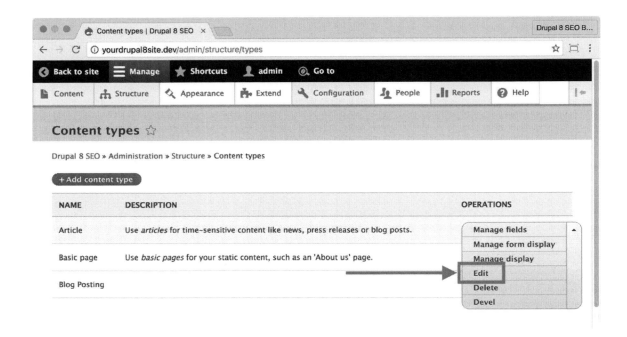

5. Next to your first Content Type, open the drop-down menu next to **Manage fields** and click **Edit**.

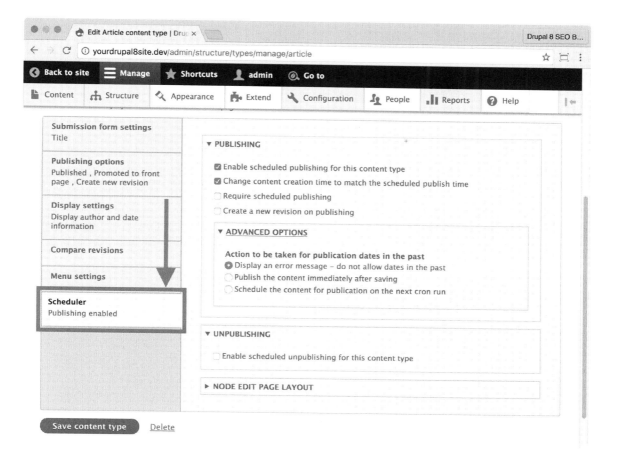

6. Click the **Scheduler** tab and select the **Enable scheduled publishing for this content type** and **Change content creation time to match the scheduled publish time** options.

7. Click the **Save content type** button at the bottom of the page.

8. Repeat steps 4-8 for the Content Types that need scheduling.

> *Tip: If you use event-related Content Types, it's a good idea to enable the Unpublishing feature of the Scheduler module. Then, you can automatically remove the event from your website after it's over.*

Using the Scheduler module

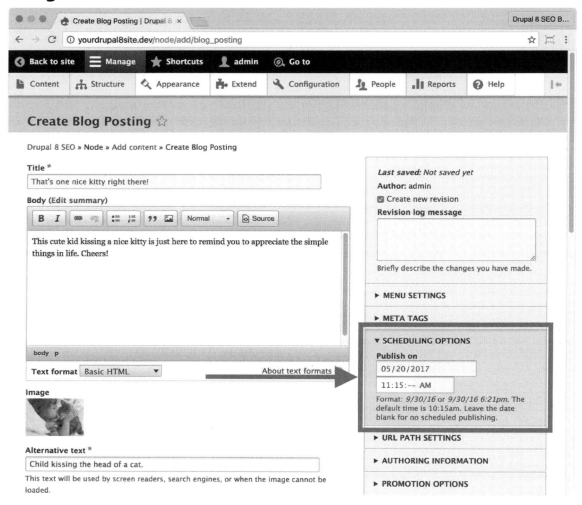

To use the *Scheduler* module, set the publishing date when you create a new piece of content and then click the **Save and publish** button. The content will be published on the next Cron run after the date and time you specify. The newly saved content will look something like this:

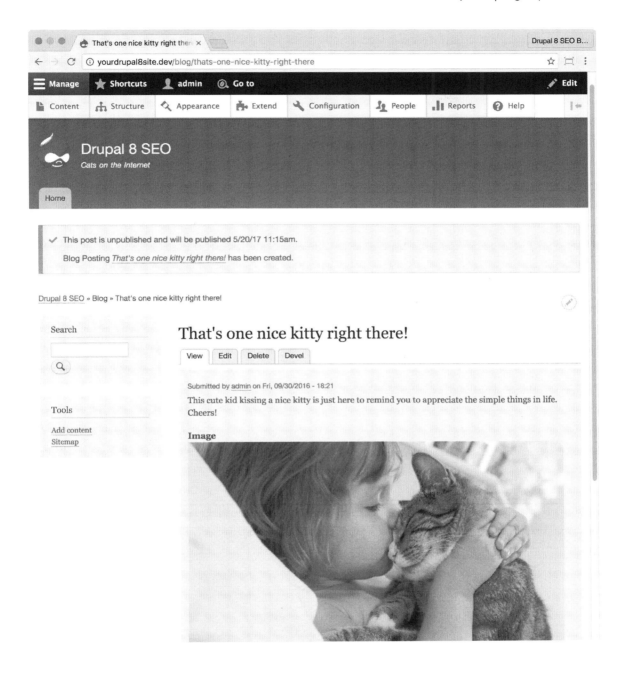

The green notification at the top tells you when it will be published. The pink highlight on the content indicates unpublished content.

Conclusion

In this chapter we covered seven *SEO Checklist* items:

- You learned how to optimize keywords on a node with the ***Yoast SEO*** module,
- You are now **tracking revisions** to your content,
- You can easily see what changed on a node with the ***Diff*** module, and
- You can publish and unpublish content on a schedule that meets your content marketing needs with the ***Scheduler*** module.

By completing these items, you can ensure properly optimized, trackable, and easily-scheduled content.

In the next chapter, we'll continue down the *SEO Checklist* with a look at the ***Security Review*** module and the ***Mollom*** module.

Chapter 9:
Security and Performance

"Protect yourself at all times."

Frankie Dunn
Million Dollar Baby

Items Covered

- Security Review module
- Mollom module
- HTTPS
- Performance admin settings
- Advanced CSS/JS Aggregation module
- Image styles
- CDNs
- Hosting

TWO KEY ATTRIBUTES OF ANY BOXER are *defense* and *quickness*. Great fighters protect themselves from attack and then quickly exploit any openings that their opponent gives them. Your website deserves similar protection.

All the great SEO in the world won't make your site great if you get hacked. There are bad people on the Internet who want to break your website, infect your visitors, steal your data, and blackmail you. From the *Panama Papers* fiasco (an old, insecure version of Drupal was in use) to your garden-variety *script kiddie*, it's apparent that you've got to invest in your defense and protect yourself and your Drupal 8 site.

The Security Review Module

https://www.drupal.org/project/security_review

Credits & Thanks

Thank you to Ben Jeavons (coltrane on Drupal.org) for creating the Security Review module. Thank you to Viktor Bán (banviktor) for your contributions.

About the Security Review Module

The *Security Review* module automatically tests for many security problems in the configuration of your Drupal site.

The *Security Review* module reviews your basic security settings and tells you if there need to be any changes to make your website more secure. More often than not, security breaches come from un-updated Core software or basic settings that are exploited and turned into a breach. If you close those holes, hackers often move on to an easier target.

☐ Install and Enable the Security Review Module

1 Install the *Security Review* module on your server. (See Chapter 1 on how to install Drupal contributed modules.)

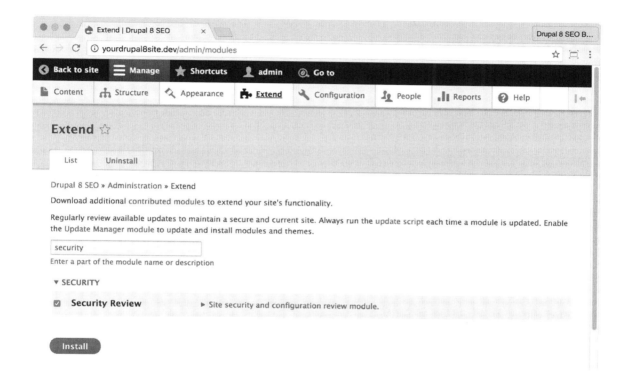

2. Go to the Extend page: Click **Manage > Extend** (Coffee: "extend") or visit `http://yourDrupal8site.dev/admin/modules` in your browser.

3. Select the checkbox next to "Security Review" and click the **Install** button at the bottom of the page.

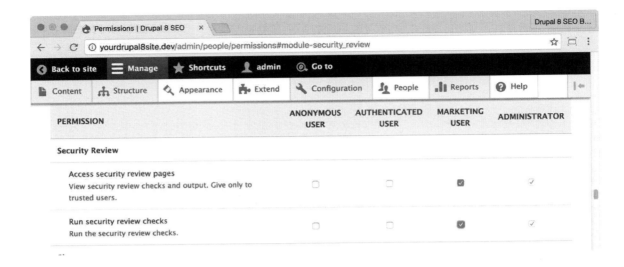

If necessary, give yourself permissions to use the Security Review module.

1. Click **Manage > People > Permissions** (Coffee: "perm") or visit
    `http://yourDrupal8site.dev/admin/people/permissions`.

2. Select the appropriate checkboxes for

    -   "Access security review pages"
    -   "Run security review checks"

3. Click the **Save permissions** button at the bottom of the page.

☐ *Configure the Security Review module*

1. Go to the *Security Review* module admin page by clicking **Manage > Reports > Security Review** (Coffee: "security") or visit `http://yourDrupal8site.dev/admin/config/security-review` in your browser.

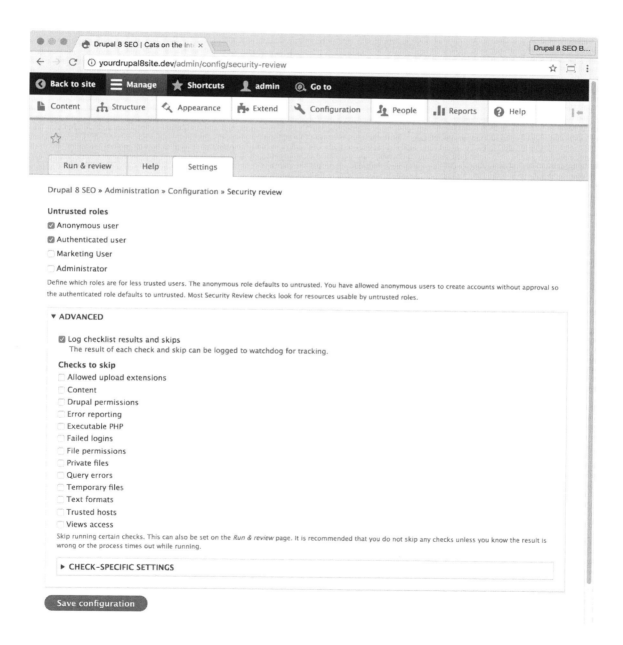

2. Set any untrusted roles. These are for typical site visitors.

3. Under Advanced, you can skip any tests that aren't appropriate for your site. If you're unsure, don't skip any of the tests.

4. Click the **Save configuration** button at the bottom of the page.

Using the Security Review module

1. Go to the *Security Review* module admin page by clicking **Manage > Reports > Security Review** (Coffee: "security") or visit `http://yourDrupal8site.dev/ admin/reports/security-review` in your browser.

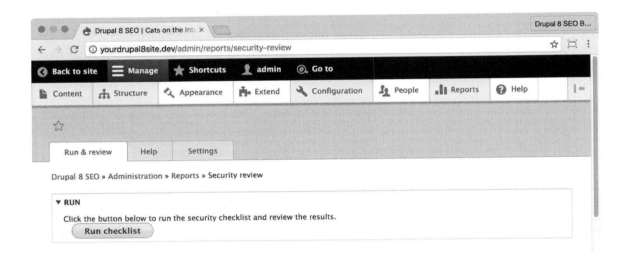

2. Click the **Run checklist** button.

3 The *Security Review* module will run. It can take several minutes

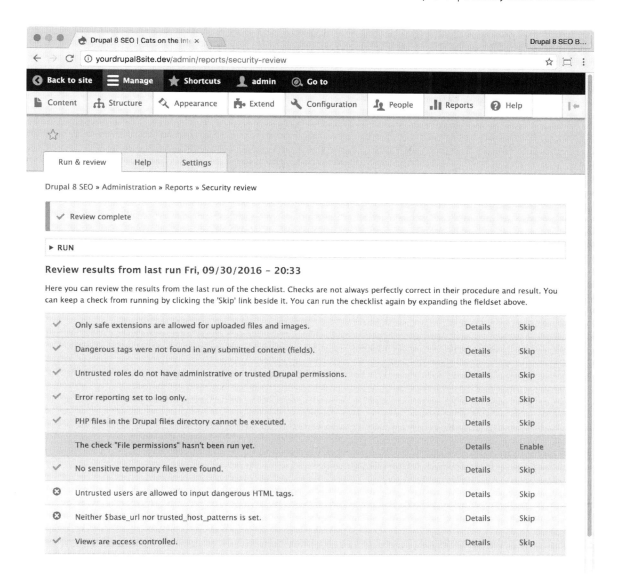

As you can see, the *Security Review* module shows where your site might be vulnerable to attack. Follow its recommendations to harden your website against malicious hackers.

The Mollom Module

https://www.drupal.org/project/mollom

Credits & Thanks

Thank you to Dries Buytaert (Dries on Drupal.org—yes that Dries Buytaert) for creating this module. Thank you to Lisa Backer (eshta) and Daniel Kudwien (sun) for their contributions.

About the Mollom module and service

> *Note: Mollom is a third party service owned by Acquia and requires you to sign up. They offer a free starter plan that you can try out.*

The *Mollom* module and service combine to create an "intelligent content moderation web service." It uses data collected from the 60,000+ websites that use the service to figure out if comments or content posted on your site are spam. If it is, it blocks it. If Mollom can't determine if it's spam or not, the module will use a Captcha and ask the submitter to prove they are a real person. Mollom boasts a 99.98% efficiency rate which means that for every 10,000 spam messages posted; only two will get through.

Spam on your website negatively affects your Google ranking. Google prefers to send visitors to non-spammy pages. Spam comments can sometimes be used to inject unwanted code into your site. Fortunately, Drupal 8 has come a long way in preventing this kind of attack. Blocking spam with Mollom is an excellent way to protect your investment in your website. If you don't use Mollom (or some other spam-prevention service), then you should carefully moderate every submission to your site—comments, content, user accounts, etc.

☐ Install and Enable the Mollom Module

1. Install the *Mollom* module on your server. (See Chapter 1 for more instructions on installing modules.)

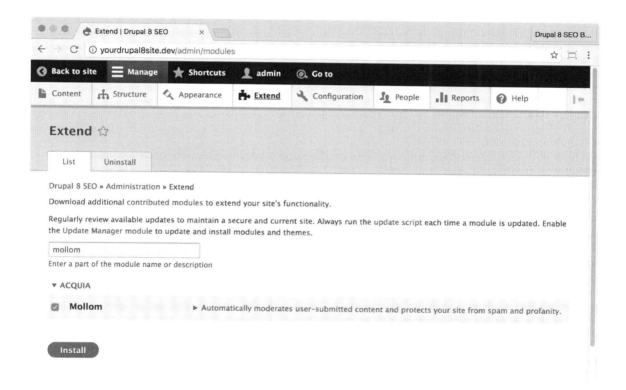

2. Go to the Extend page: Click **Manage > Extend** (Coffee: "extend") or visit `http://yourDrupal8site.dev/admin/modules` in your browser.

3. Select the checkbox next to "Mollom" and click the **Install** button at the bottom of the page.

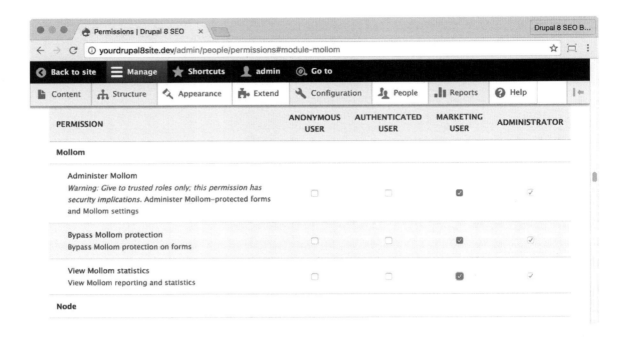

If necessary, give yourself permissions to use the *Mollom* module.

1. Click **Manage > People > Permissions** (Coffee: "perm") or visit `http://yourDrupal8site.dev/admin/people/permissions`.

2. Select the appropriate checkboxes for

    -   "Administer Mollom"
    -   "Bypass Mollom protection"
    -   "View Mollom statistics".

3. Click the **Save permissions** button at the bottom of the page.

☐ *Sign up for the Mollom service*

1. Go to https://www.mollom.com/pricing and pick a plan. You can try the service out before buying with Mollom Free. It will handle up to 50 legit posts per day—enough for a small website.

2. Add your site to Mollom site manager.

3. Click "View keys" on the Mollom site.

4. Leave that window open so you can copy and paste those keys into the *Mollom* module.

☐ *Configure the Mollom module*

1. Go to the Mollom module admin page by clicking **Manage > Configuration > Content authoring > Mollom content moderation** (Coffee: "mollom") or visit `http://yourDrupal8site.dev/admin/config/content/mollom/settings` in your browser.

2. Click on the **Settings** tab on the *Mollom* module admin page.

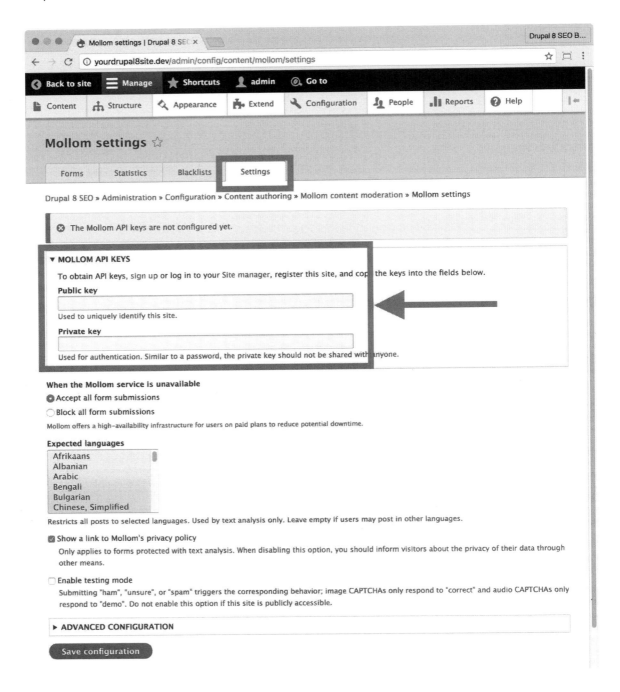

3. Copy and paste the **Public key** and **Private key** from Mollom.com into your *Mollom* module admin settings page.

   A. Paste the Public key into the **Public key** field.

        B.   Paste the Private key into the **Private key** field.

4.   Select your site's languages in the **Expected languages** field.

5.   Click the **Save configuration** button at the bottom of the page.

Now, let's protect your forms.

6.   Click the **Forms** tab.

7.   Click "Mollom Form" and select a form that your site uses.

8. The default options usually work well.

9. Click the **Create Protected Mollom Form** button.

10. Repeat steps 6-9 for the rest of the forms that your site uses.

Test Mollom. View one of the forms you added in an incognito window. Use words like "viagra", "refinance", and "enlargement" and add a link or two. Try to submit the form and see what happens.

☐ Secure Your Website with HTTPS

SEO Training Camp
https://webmasters.googleblog.com/2014/08/https-as-ranking-signal.html

HTTPS (HyperText Transport Protocol Secure) is how servers send encrypted web pages to visitors' browsers. What does this have to do with SEO?

In June 2014, Google called for "HTTPS everywhere" on the web. They then began testing out using secure, HTTPS websites as a ranking signal. You're reading that right: If your website is secured using HTTPS with at least a 2048-bit key certificate, Google will rank you higher in their search results.

> *Note: For years HTTPS was mainly used for eCommerce sites and the contact-us form because the encryption and decryption created too much server overhead which slowed the site down. With today's fast processors, it's unnoticeable.*

You secure your website by installing an SSL certificate and adjusting your DNS and server settings. It can be a complicated process and differs depending on your server software, hosting company, and many other factors. Consult your web hosting company for the exact details. The process will look something like this:

1. Buy an SSL Certificate from an issuing authority. I use *GoDaddy*, but there are many other issuers like *DigiCert* or *GlobalSign*. Check with your hosting company to see if they can give you specific recommendations.

   A. You'll typically use a single-domain certificate, but you can use multi-domain or wildcard certificate.

   B. I recommend an **EV** (Extended Validation) **SSL Certificate** as it provides a visible green address bar as feedback to your site's visitors that the site is secure. It's not required, though—a standard certificate will work for SEO purposes.

   C. The process involves proving to the issuing authority that you control the domain name in your request. The process usually takes from one to seven days and you may be asked to provide information about your business.

2. After you receive your certificate, contact your hosting company and request that they install it on your server. They may ask you to get a pre-configured version of the certificate for your particular server software. Apache is the most common but ask your hosting company. You'll get the specially-configured certificate from the issuing authority.

3. During testing, you'll be able to access your website at both **http**://yourDrupal8site.dev and **https**://yourDrupal8site.dev. Make sure you thoroughly test forms and the checkout process.

4. Google Search Console

   A. Verify the HTTPS version of your site with **Google Search Console**. (See Chapter 5.) Make sure that you verify both the HTTP and HTTPS version of your website.

B. Submit the HTTPS version of your XML Sitemap to Google Search Console.

5. When you're ready to make the switch to HTTPS, ask your hosting company (or your server admin) to redirect HTTP queries to HTTPS.

6. Monitor your traffic in Google Search Console. Pay particular attention to the Index Status and Crawl Errors.

> *Tip: Google has published a step-by-step process that provides useful information for migrating websites to HTTPS. See https://support.google.com/webmasters/answer/6033049?utm _source=wmx_blog&utm_medium=referral&utm_campaign=tl s_en_post*

Now that your site is more secure let's make sure it's running as fast as possible.

☐ Adjust Performance Admin Settings

Drupal 8 enables caching by default for anonymous visitors. That is sufficient for small to medium-sized websites with moderate traffic. You can turn it off for development purposes by setting it to "<no caching>". Be sure to turn it back on before you launch or your site will be slow.

1. Go to the Performance admin page by clicking **Manage > Configuration > Development > Performance** (Coffee: "performance") or visit `http://yourDrupal8site.dev/admin/config/development/performance` in your browser.

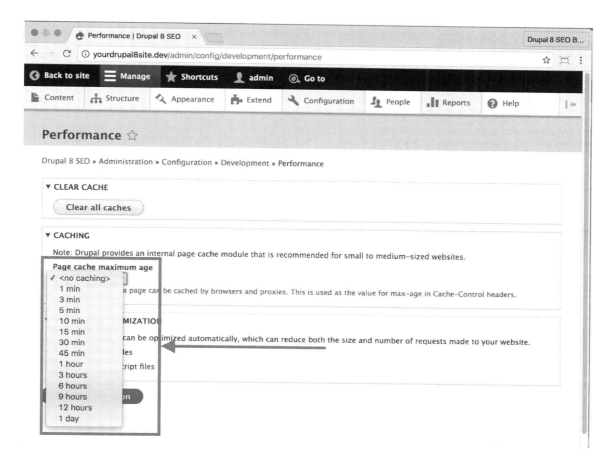

2. You need to make a judgment call on Page caching maximum age. How quickly does your website content change? Every fifteen minutes? Every hour? Daily?

      A. 1 day—for websites that are only updated a couple of times per week. There is no commenting or other interaction on the site. (e.g. lead generation brochure site)

      B. 1 hour—for websites that are updated once or twice per day. (e.g. eCommerce)

      C. 15 minutes—for frequently updated websites. (e.g. news sites)

3. Under "Bandwidth Optimization", make sure "Aggregate CSS files" and "Aggregate JavaScript files" are both selected.

4. Click the **Save configuration** button.

5. If you use Views or Panels, you can get more fine-grained in your cache settings. The caching on each block can be customized as well.

The Advanced CSS/JS Aggregation Module

https://www.drupal.org/project/advagg

Credits & Thanks

Thank you to Mike Carper (mikeytown2 on Drupal.org) for creating and maintaining this module. Thank you to Nick Wilde (NickWilde) for his contributions to improving Drupal's response times.

About the Advanced CSS/JS Aggregation Module

The *Advanced CSS/JS Aggregation* module aggregates and compresses CSS and JavaScript files to make your site run faster. Speed became a ranking factor in April of 2010. All else being equal, the faster site will rank higher in Google. Making your site as fast as you reasonably can will benefit your marketing efforts.

Google loves fast websites, and this module speeds up Drupal 8.

Before you install and use this module, take a few minutes and use Google's PageSpeed Insights tool (https://developers.google.com/speed/pagespeed/insights/) and WebPageTest.org (http://www.webpagetest.org/) to take a benchmark of how your website performs.

Print or record your scores as they'll come in handy later for comparison.

☐ *Install and Enable the Advanced CSS/JS Aggregation Module*

> **Warning: You might want to work with your developer on this! Try things out on a dev server before you push it to your live website. Mistakes can bring down your website.**

1. Install the *Advanced CSS/JS Aggregation* module on your server. (See Chapter 1 for more instructions on installing modules.)

2. Go to the Extend page: Click **Manage > Extend** (Coffee: "extend") or visit `http://yourDrupal8site.dev/admin/modules` in your browser.

3. Select the checkboxes next to:

    A. AdvAgg Bundler

    B. AdvAgg CDN

    C. AdvAgg CSS/JS Validator

    D. AdvAgg External Minification

    E. AdvAgg Minify CSS

    F. AdvAgg Minify JavaScript

    G. AdvAgg Modifier

    H. Advanced CSS/JS Aggregation

4. Click the **Install** button at the bottom of the page.

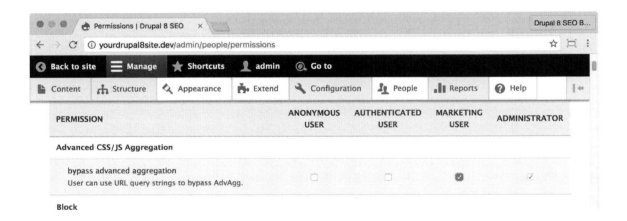

If necessary, give yourself permissions to use the *Advanced CSS/JS Aggregation* module.

1. Click **Manage > People > Permissions** (Coffee: "perm") or visit `http://yourDrupal8site.dev/admin/people/permissions`.

2. Select the appropriate checkbox for "bypass advanced aggregation".

3. Click the **Save permissions** button at the bottom of the page.

☐ Configure the Advanced CSS/JS Aggregation module

> *Warning in advance: There are a lot of options for this module. If you run into CSS or JavaScript issues with your site, a setting in this module may be the problem. Be sure to work closely with your developer and website admin to get the settings right.*

1. Go to the *Advanced CSS/JS Aggregation* module admin page by clicking **Manage > Configuration > Development > Performance > AdvAgg** (Coffee: "advagg") or visit `http://yourDrupal8site.dev//config/development/performance/advagg` in your browser.

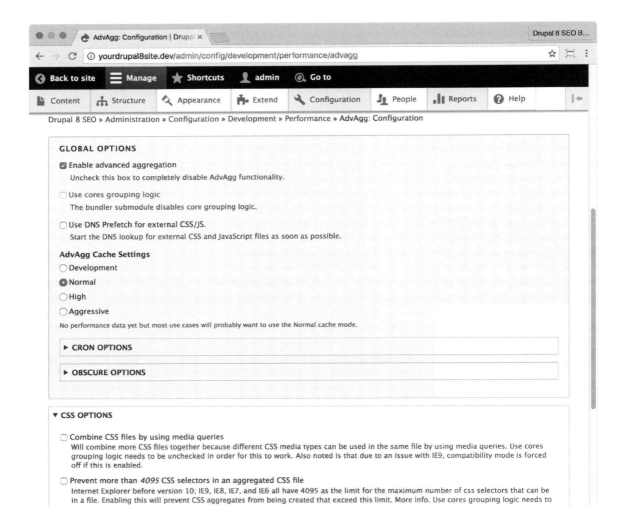

2. To start out, **don't change anything!** The default settings for this module are pretty spot-on for error free performance.

3. Test your site. Make sure all of your pages are loading properly.

4. You can squeeze faster performance out of your website by testing the High and Aggressive settings. Just be aware that they may cause some pages to display incorrectly. As with all things, check your results thoroughly.

JavaScript Minification

"Minification (also minimisation or minimization), in computer programming languages and especially JavaScript, is the process of removing all unnecessary characters from source code without changing its functionality. These unnecessary characters usually include white space characters, new line characters, comments, and sometimes block delimiters, which are used to add readability to the code but are not required for it to execute." —Wikipedia

By default, Advanced CSS/JS Aggregation does not minify **JavaScript** files. You can turn on Minification like this:

1. Go to the *Advanced CSS/JS Aggregation* module admin page by clicking **Manage > Configuration > Development > Performance > AdvAgg > JavaScript Minification** (Coffee: "javascript") or visit `http://yourDrupal8site.dev//config/development/performance/advagg/js-minify` in your browser.

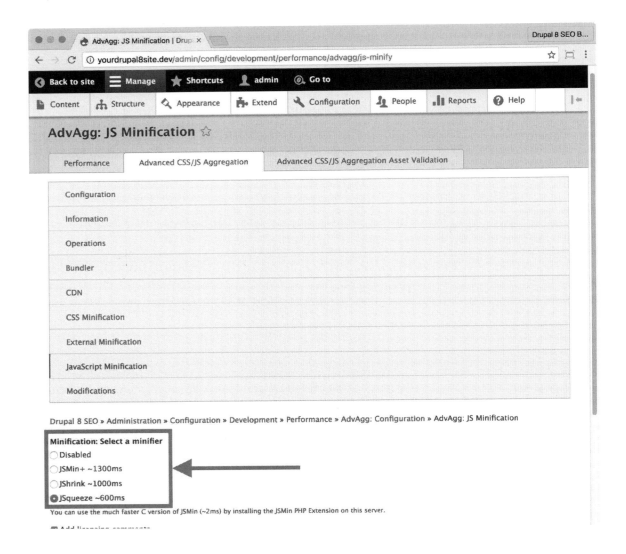

2. There are 3 built-in options. Select **JSqueeze**.

3. Click the **Save configuration** button at the bottom of the page.

4. Test! Make sure your site is working properly. Be sure to check all of your contact forms.

Take a post-installation benchmark with Google's PageSpeed Insights tool (https://developers.google.com/speed/pagespeed/insights/) and WebPageTest.org (http://www.webpagetest.org/). These tools will help you determine if more aggressive caching will improve your site's speed.

Controlling Image Bandwidth with Image Styles

Drupal 8 Core can resize images and serve the right image for any situation. It can scale them, crop them, and much more. Consistent image sizes reduce the bandwidth required and decreases load time.

> *SEO Training Camp*
> * *https://www.ostraining.com/blog/drupal/image-styles/*
> * *Facebook provides <u>recommendations</u> for minimum image sizes for your content to look good on any device. We'll use their suggestions here. (See <u>https://developers.facebook.com/docs/sharing/best-practices#images</u>.)*

☐ *Configure Image Styles*

1. Go to the Image Styles admin page by clicking **Manage > Configuration > Media > Image styles** (Coffee: "image styles") or visit `http://yourDrupal8site.dev/admin/config/media/image-styles` in your browser.

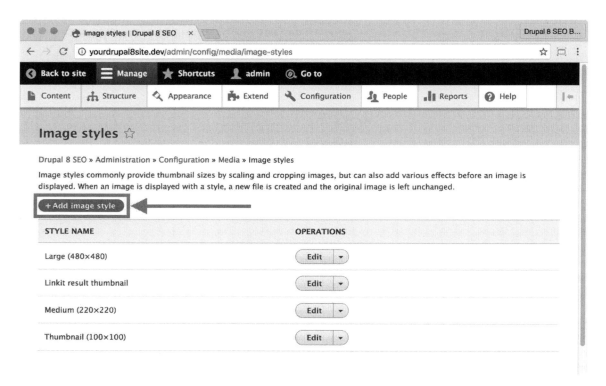

2. Click the **+Add image style** button.

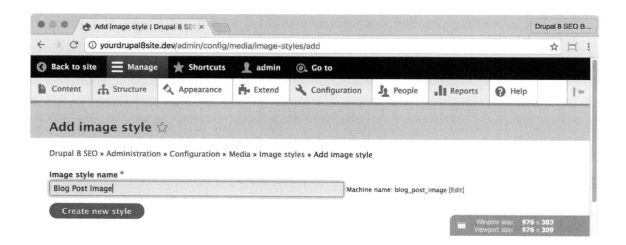

3. Enter a name for your new style and click the **Create new style** button.

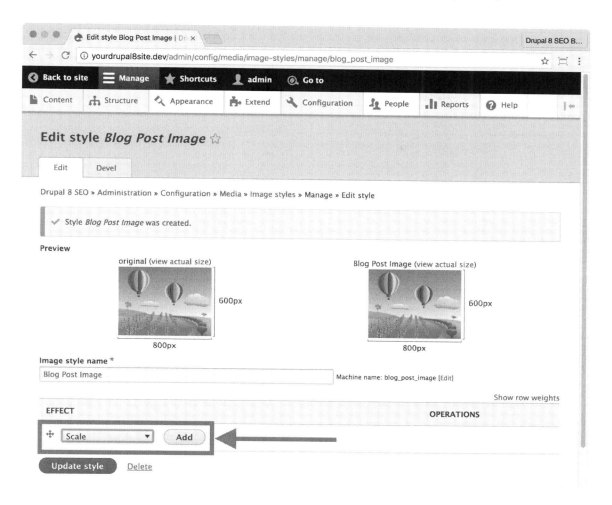

4. Under **Effect**, select **Scale** from the drop-down and click the **Add** button.

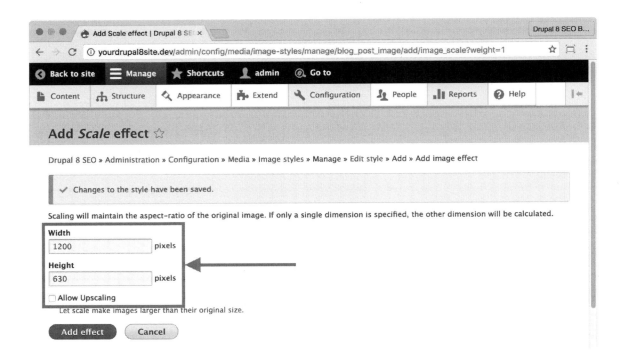

5. Enter the maximum allowable dimensions for the image. In this case, we'll use 1200 x 630. Leave "allow upscaling" unchecked.

6. Click the **Add effect** button.

Applying the new image style to your blog

Now that you've created a great new style let's apply it to your blog.

1. Go to the Blog posting admin page by clicking **Manage > Structure > Content Types** and click the **Manage fields** button (Coffee: "blog postings") or visit
`http://yourDrupal8site.dev/admin/structure/types/manage/blog_posting` in your browser.

2. Click the **Manage display** tab.

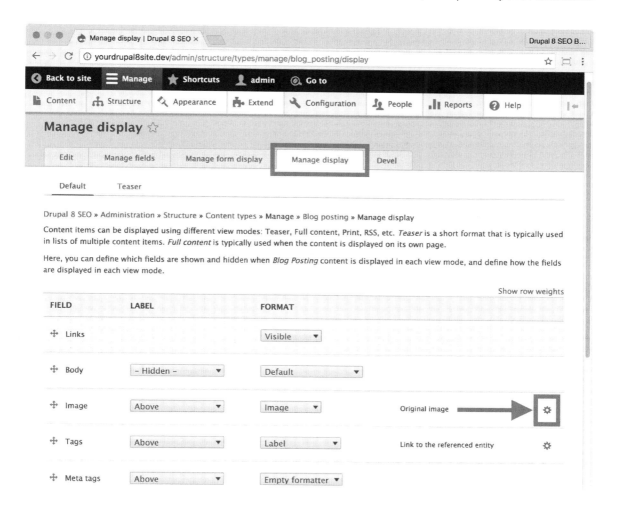

3. Click the gear icon next to the Image field.

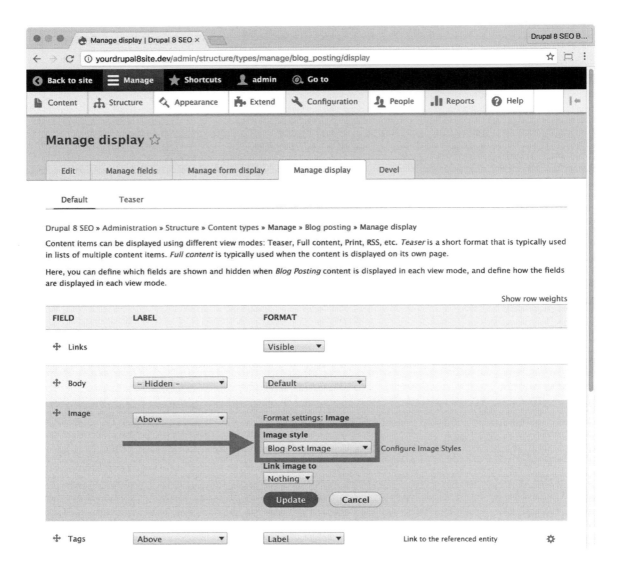

4. For Image style, select the new image style you just created.

5. Click the **Update** button.

6. Click the **Save** button.

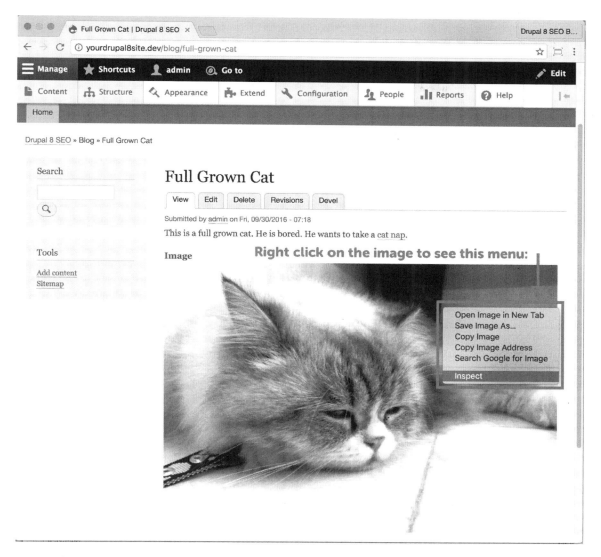

To verify that it worked, go to any blog post. Right click on the main image and select "Inspect".

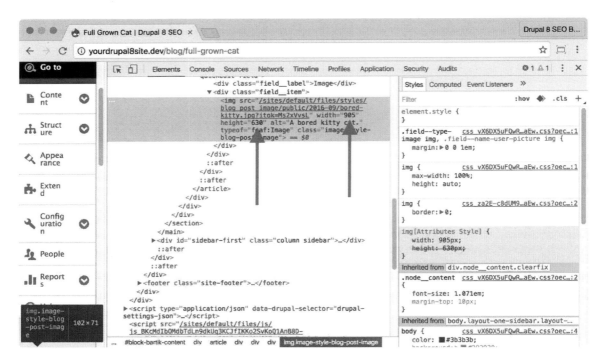

You'll see that the scaled image is displayed.

You can do the same with each Content Type, user photos, etc.

Third Party Speed Options

There are a few third-party tools that you can use with Drupal to speed up your website. I mention them here to show you the possibilities.

> **Warning: Configuring these options can be technical. It's best to work closely with your developer and hosting company to find the right solution.**

☐ Set up a CDN

A CDN, or "Content Distribution Network" stores a cache of your website on servers across the globe. CDN companies own data centers on every continent and in every region. Think of it as taking your server cache and making copies of it to servers that are a lot closer to your visitors—in both a physical and network sense. If the HTML does not need to be recreated by Drupal, then it is served directly from the CDN, significantly reducing the load times involved.

Example companies include (my personal favorite) CloudFlare, Level3, Amazon, and Akamai. The CDN module for Drupal can be downloaded at https://www.drupal.org/project/cdn. There are also service-specific modules for CloudFlare - https://www.drupal.org/project/cloudflare and Akamai - https://www.drupal.org/project/akamai.

☐ Move to Fast Hosting

If you've done the recommendations in this chapter and your site still takes longer than two seconds to load; it may be time to look for better hosting. When you look for hosting, you'll find many options. At Volacci, we have experience with dozens of hosting companies that promise Drupal support and high speeds. In order of most capable to least capable (with considerable overlap in performance and cost), here is a list of the types of hosting you may want to consider:

Managed Dedicated Server(s)

Managed dedicated server takes care of all your hosting needs for you. Not only do you get the hardware but also a team of experts who make sure everything is running as it should. They will keep your software up-to-date and alert you if there are any problems—often after they've already fixed the issue. You can deploy multiple servers in many configurations. For example, a firewall, caching server, database server or multiple HTTP servers could all be part of a complete hosting solution. It's fast and reliable hosting. Adding multiple servers or getting help designing the perfect configuration for you is part of the service. Blackmesh (my personal favorite) is the Drupal-specific company for this kind of hosting.

Dedicated Server(s)

A dedicated server provides low latency which means a fast response time for most small to medium-sized sites. Consider that you need to provide your own technical staff to manage the hardware and software stack. Examples include HostGator and Viawest.

Cloud Hosting

Cloud hosting is scalable. The "cloud" means that there is a data center with lots of dormant servers. As your site's needs scale up (or down), the servers in the data center spin up to provide you with more server power. While it may be a panacea for some, latency and cost are critical concerns. Examples include Acquia Cloud, Pantheon, and Platform.sh.

> *Note: Platform.sh allows command line access to your site and can host many different technologies including Drupal. Pantheon focuses on Drupal and WordPress. Acquia Cloud is Drupal-only.*

Virtual Private Server (VPS) / Server Slice

A VPS offers a good balance between cost and performance. It's similar to shared hosting in that you share a single server with other tenants. However, you get a guaranteed amount of performance on that server—maybe 10% (or more) dedicated to you—which helps preserve your performance when someone else's site gets busy. Examples include HotDrupal and Green VPS.

Shared Hosting

Shared hosting is the rookie league of hosting. Your site sits on a server with many other tenants. It's slow and not scalable, but it's inexpensive. Examples include Bluehost and SiteGround.

Conclusion

In this chapter we covered twelve *SEO Checklist* items that are related to security or speed:

- You've fixed any holes in your site's security with the **Security Review** module,
- You're blocking Spam with the **Mollom** module.
- Your website is transmitting securely to users' browsers with **HTTPS**,
- Your website is performing faster because you set **Performance admin settings**,
- Data is flowing quickly because you installed the **Advanced CSS/JS Aggregation**, module,
- You're sending correctly-sized images by setting up **Image styles**,
- Your site is getting to your visitors faster because you're using a **CDN**, and finally
- Your site is more responsive because you've upgraded your hosting.

By completing these items, you can be sure that your site speed is as fast as it reasonably can be. Security and speed are staples of great Google rankings.

In the next chapter, we'll continue down the *SEO Checklist* with a look at mobile and social tools for Drupal 8 SEO.

Chapter 10: Mobile & Social

"Going in one more round when you don't think you can, that's what makes all the difference in your life."

Rocky Balboa
Rocky IV

Items Covered

- Responsive design
- *AMP* module
- *AMP* theme
- *AMP* PHP library
- *AddToAny* module

ROCKY TOOK A BEATING in fight after fight. He got knocked down, trod on, and had the heart to get back up and keep going. Great marketers are the same way. There is a mountain of SEO work to be done on your site, and here you are in Chapter 10 getting them done. Kudos! Your patience will be rewarded. Don't worry; only a few items remain before your technical SEO journey is complete.

In this chapter, we are going to cover the most important aspects of mobile SEO: Responsive Design and the Accelerated Mobile Pages (AMP). We're then going to tackle basic Social optimization. These final tasks will make all the difference in your Drupal 8 site.

Check Site for Responsive Web Design

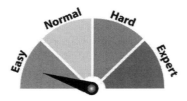

Responsive, mobile-first web design is the default design methodology in Drupal 8. That's good because Google specifically states that they prefer it when serving mobile devices. (See https://developers.google.com/webmasters/mobile-sites/mobile-seo/.) When using responsive design, the server sends the same HTML code to each device. CSS is then used to change the way the page looks based on the size of the screen. It allows a single URL to be used for the same content, and that's ideal for sharing and offering up pages to your visitors.

☐ *Make sure your site is responsive*

There are a couple of ways to check for responsive design on your website.

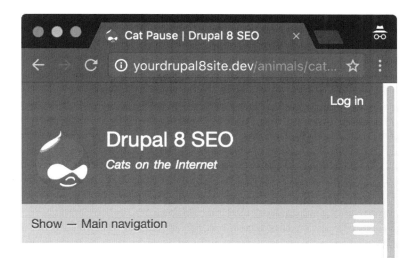

Drupal 8 SEO » Animals » Cats » Cat Pause

Cat Pause

Submitted by admin on Wed, 09/28/2016 - 06:46

A mother cat and her kitten take a break for a quick cat nap. Kittens sleep almost 20 hours per day while full grown cats will only sleep about 16 hours daily. Like their big cat cousins, cats store up energy so that they can pounce on their prey.

Image

Tags
cute cats

Open an incognito window and shrink it down to size. How does it look? Are the images scaled nicely?

Open your site on your smartphone. Again, check the images, check the layout. How does it look?

Third party services that can help here:

- http://whatismyscreenresolution.net/multi-screen-test allows you to try many different screen sizes in one web interface.
- Google's Mobile-Friendly Test: https://www.google.com/webmasters/tools/mobile-friendly/ will test a single page for specific mobile-friendly action items.
- Google Search Console (see Chapter 5) has a **Search Traffic > Mobile Usability** section that shows how individual pages of your website are doing for mobile.

If your site is not responsive, you need a responsive theme. Discuss the possibilities with your designer, themer, and developer.

AMP – Accelerated Mobile Pages

"The Accelerated Mobile Pages (AMP) Project is an open source initiative that embodies the vision that publishers can create mobile optimized content once and have it load instantly everywhere."

Accelerated Mobile Pages Project

https://www.ampproject.org/

Google announced the AMP project in October of 2015. In April the following year Google announced that they would give higher placement to articles in Google News that use the AMP standard. While the standard is relatively new, some believe that more and more of Google's listings will reward publishers that use AMP. In fact, on August 2, 2016, Google announced expanded support for the AMP format in the entire search results pages.

By building AMP into your website, you enable Google and other websites to store specially formatted versions of your content on their servers. That means that any mobile users will be served a streamlined version of your content nearly instantly. It's similar to how a CDN works, but it's specific to mobile.

> *SEO Training Camp*
> - *https://www.ampproject.org/how-it-works/*
> - *https://webmasters.googleblog.com/2016/08/amp-your-content-preview-of-amped.html)*

Drupal AMP Module, Theme, & PHP Library Suite

https://www.drupal.org/project/amp

https://www.drupal.org/project/amptheme

https://github.com/Lullabot/amp-library

Credits & Thanks

Thank you to the Drupal AMP team which consists of Marc Drummond (mdrummond on Drupal.org), Matthew Tift (mtift), and Sidharth Kshatriya (sidharth_k) and to the Lullabot company for supporting this project.

About the AMP Suite for Drupal

The *AMP* Suite converts Drupal pages into AMP-compliant pages. This conversion makes your pages available to any service that serves AMP pages to visitors, such as Google News and Google search results.

In February of 2016, the Drupal community, led by Lullabot, released the Drupal 8 *AMP* module to provide support for AMP for the Drupal project. They did an excellent job of describing how it works in a blog post here: https://www.lullabot.com/articles/amping-up-drupal:

> "When the *AMP* module is installed, AMP can be enabled for any content type. At that point, a new AMP view mode is created for that content type, and AMP content becomes available on URLs such as node/1/amp or node/article-

title/amp. We also created special AMP formatters for text, image, and video fields.

"The *AMP* theme is designed to produce the very specific markup that the AMP HTML standard requires. The *AMP* theme is triggered for any node delivered on an /amp path. As with any Drupal theme, the *AMP* theme can be extended using a subtheme, allowing publishers as much flexibility as they need to customize how AMP pages are displayed. This also makes it possible to do things like place AMP ad blocks on the AMP page using Drupal's block system.

"The PHP Library analyzes HTML entered by users into rich text fields and reports issues that might make the HTML non-compliant with the AMP standard. The library does its best to make corrections to the HTML, where possible, and automatically converts images and iframes into their AMP HTML equivalents. More automatic conversions will be available in the future."

☐ *Install and Enable the AMP Suite*

1. Installing the *AMP* Suite requires the use of **Composer**. This must be done at the command line so ask your developer for help if you need it.

> A. The commands typically are:
> >composer require drupal/amp
> >composer require drupal/amptheme

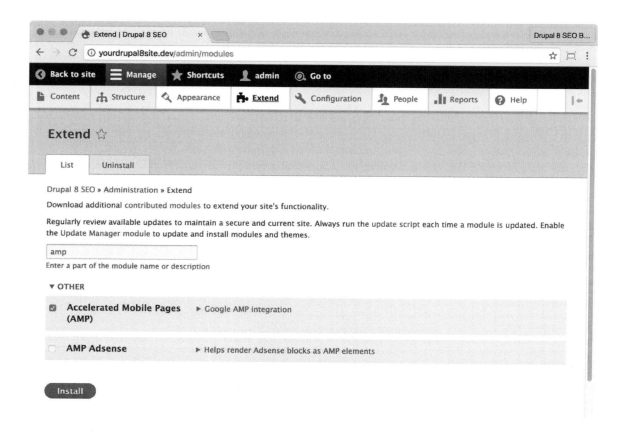

2. Go to the Extend page: Click **Manage > Extend** (Coffee: "extend") or visit `http://yourDrupal8site.dev/admin/modules` in your browser.

3. Select the checkbox next to "Accelerated Mobile Pages (AMP)" and click the **Install** button at the bottom of the page.

There are no separate permissions required for the *AMP* module.

☐ *Install the AMP themes*

1. Go to the Appearance admin page by clicking **Manage > Appearance** (Coffee: "appearance") or visit `http://yourDrupal8site.dev/admin/appearance` in your browser.

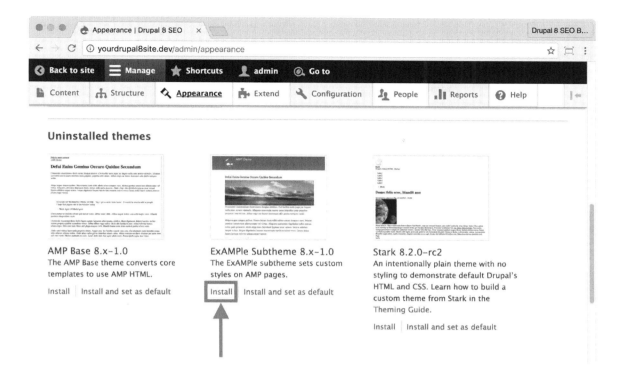

2. Click the **Install** link below ExAMPle Subtheme.

☐ *Configure AMP*

1. Go to the *AMP* module admin page by clicking **Manage > Content authoring > AMP Configuration** (Coffee: "amp") or visit `http://yourDrupal8site.dev/admin/config/content/amp` in your browser.

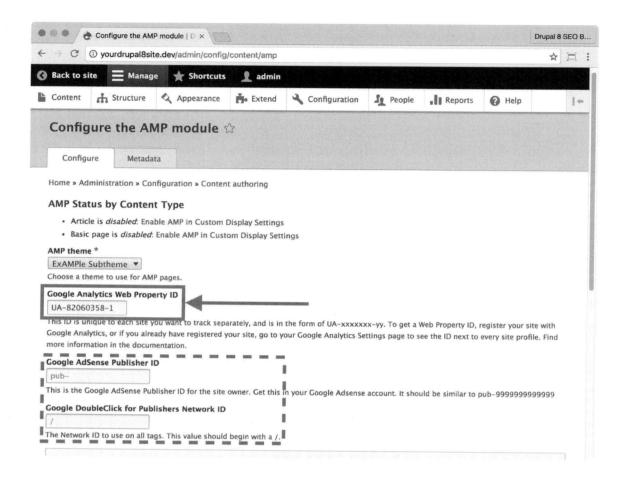

2. Configure the module as shown above:

> A. Under **AMP theme**, select ExAMPle Subtheme.

> B. Enter your **Google Analytics Web Property ID** which can be found in your *Google Analytics* module settings (coffee: "Google Analytics") or by logging in to Google Analytics and visiting Admin > Property Settings > Tracking ID.

> C. If you use AdSense or Doubleclick, enter their respective numbers in the fields provided.

3. Click the **Save configuration** button at the bottom of the page.

Enable AMP for each Content Type

1. Go to the *AMP* module admin page by clicking **Manage > Content authoring > AMP Configuration** (Coffee: "amp") or visit
    `http://yourDrupal8site.dev/admin/config/content/amp` in your browser.

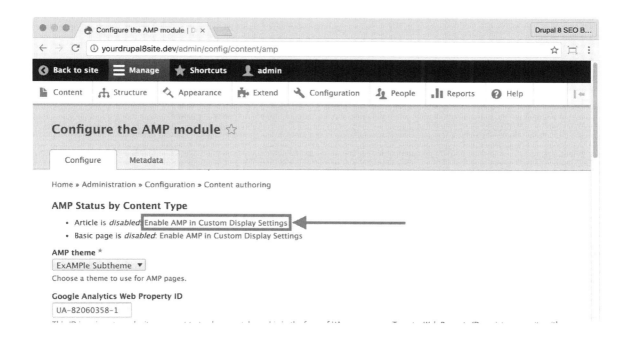

2. Click "Enable AMP in Custom Display Settings" link

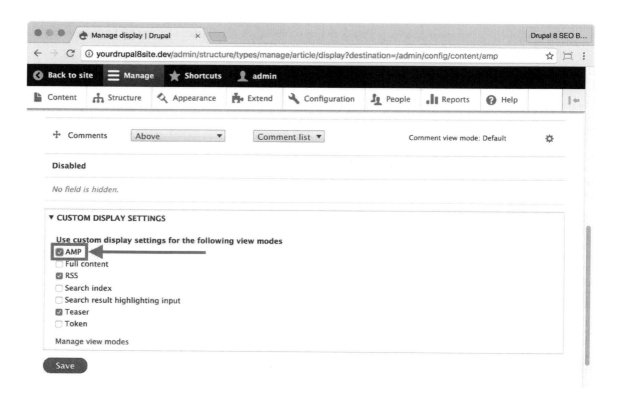

3. On the following page, open the "Custom Display Settings" drop down.

4. Select the "AMP" checkbox.

5. Click the **Save** button at the bottom of the page.

6. Repeat steps 1-5 for each Content Type that will use AMP.

Configure display blocks for the AMP theme

You can see the AMP version of your pages by adding "?amp" to the end of any node that you've set up in this way. You may see a lot of extra blocks in the header that pushes your content down below the fold. You can rearrange the blocks or remove them from the theme. In this example, we'll go with the ExAMPle sub-theme but this works on any theme.

1. Go to the **ExAMPle subtheme Block layout** admin page by clicking **Manage > Structure > Block layout** and then clicking ExAMPle Subtheme (Coffee: "block") or visit

http://yourDrupal8site.dev/admin/structure/block/list/ampsub
theme_example in your browser.

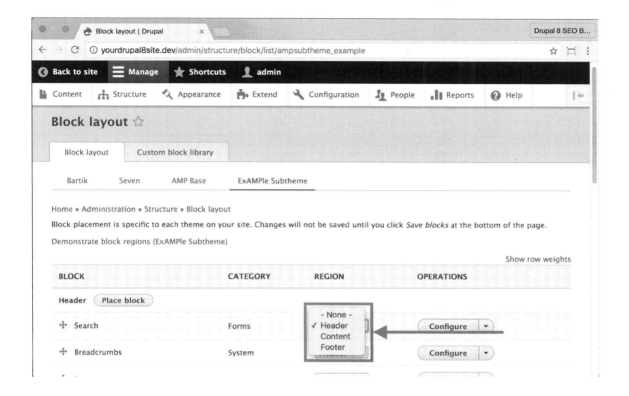

2. In the **Region** column next to each Block, change the drop-down from "Header" to "Footer" or "None". Header blocks appear at the top, Footer blocks at the bottom, and None will be hidden on this theme.

3. Click the **Save blocks** button at the bottom of the page.

Take another look at your AMP pages. They should look cleaner and easier to read.

Validate AMP pages

1. Go to one of your AMP pages on your website.

2. View source and copy the HTML.

3. Visit https://validator.ampproject.org/

4. Paste in the HTML.

5. The site will give you inline error reporting alongside the HTML source of the page.

Now, you wait for Google to crawl your website. The Googlebot will automatically detect that you have AMP compatible pages. After you added AMP and Google has crawled your website, you can validate your AMP pages using Google Search Console: https://www.google.com/webmasters/tools/accelerated-mobile-pages

The Share Buttons by AddToAny Module

https://www.drupal.org/project/addtoany

Credits & Thanks

Thank you to Patrick Przybilla (patPrzybilla on Drupal.org) for creating and maintaining the *Share Buttons by AddToAny* module.

About the Share Buttons by AddToAny Module

The *Share Buttons by AddToAny* module adds SVG sharing icons for Drupal including a universal share button, Facebook, Twitter, Google+, Pinterest, WhatsApp, and many more.

☐ *Install and Enable the Share Buttons by AddToAny Module*

1. Install the *Share Buttons by AddToAny* module on your server. (See Chapter 1 for more instructions on installing modules.)

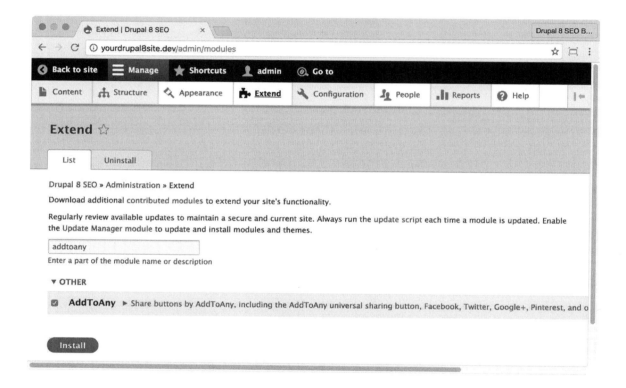

2. Go to the Extend page: Click **Manage > Extend** (Coffee: "extend") or visit `http://yourDrupal8site.dev/admin/modules` in your browser.

3. Select the checkbox next to "AddToAny" and click the **Install** button at the bottom of the page.

There are no separate permissions required for the *Share Buttons by AddToAny* module.

☐ *Configure the Share Buttons by AddToAny module*

1. Go to the *Share Buttons by AddToAny* module admin page by clicking **Manage > Configuration > System > AddToAny** (Coffee: "addto") or visit `http://yourDrupal8site.dev/admin/config/system/addtoany` in your browser.

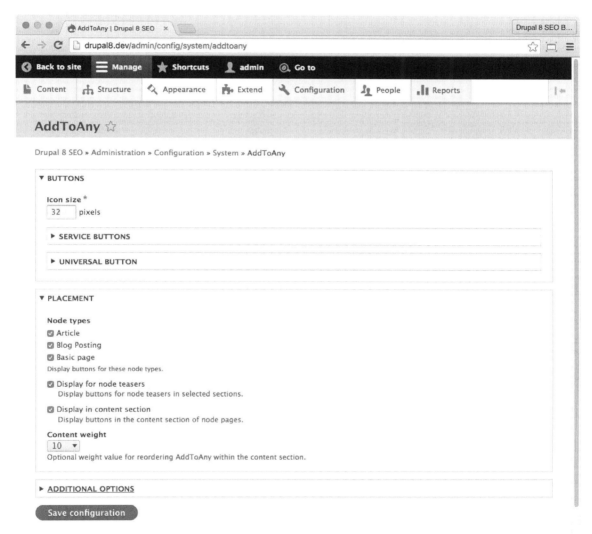

2. Configure the module as shown above. Be sure to select each of the Content Types on which you wish to display the AddToAny buttons.

3. Click the **Save configuration** button at the bottom of the page.

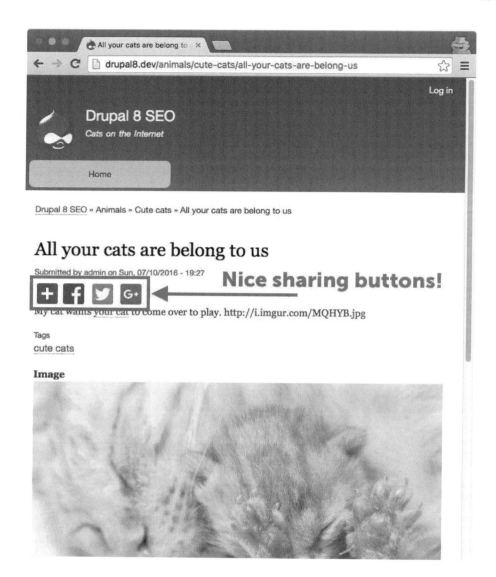

As you can see, the *Share Buttons by AddToAny* module adds some nice-looking sharing buttons to your content. These buttons make it easy for your visitors to share on social media.

Conclusion

In this chapter we covered five *SEO Checklist* items:

- You checked your site to make sure it is using **responsive design**,
- You set up **Drupal's *AMP* suite** to accelerate mobile pages in Google, and
- You installed the ***Share Buttons by AddToAny*** module making it a snap to share your content on social websites.

These tasks will make sure your website works well and loads fast for mobile devices. You're now utilizing Google's AMP specification which can help increase your visibility in search results. Finally, with *Share Buttons by AddToAny*, you're making your content easy to share for your visitors.

Index

Thank you for buying

Drupal 8 SEO

If you enjoyed this book, please consider leaving a review on Amazon.com, Barnes & Noble, Goodreads, or wherever fine books and ebooks are sold. If you prefer to give private feedback, please email ben+drupal8seo@volacci.com. Your reviews are encouraging and helps me to write better books. Thank you!

About Volacci

Volacci is a team of professionals dedicated to making marketing with Drupal easier and more effective. We advance Drupal in two ways: creating critical resources (like this book), and providing Drupal marketing services. We work with businesses of all shapes and sizes—from startups to large enterprises.

Are you curious if Volacci can help? Contact us: sales@volacci.com or visit our website to find out more: https://www.Volacci.com/.

—An Excerpt from the Volacci Blog—

10 Reasons That You Need Drupal SEO (instead of just plain ol' SEO)

Because you want marketing results faster, easier, and better.

You've made a significant resource investment to get Drupal running just the way it should. Now you need results fast. Volacci can help:

1. Faster—Our unique Drupal knowledge accelerates marketing results. We get your optimizations done quicker and better than anyone else.

2. Easier—We speak in a language you may already understand, like Nodes, Views, Blocks, Themes, and Modules. A common understanding means clearer communication and better outcomes.

3. Efficient—We work with many of the top Drupal companies so we may already have relationships with your developer, themer, and hosting company. That trust helps your project move forward more efficiency.

4. Tools—Drupal is a sophisticated system that requires special tools to make it hum. We have the tools - in fact, we helped build them.

5. Better—We give back to Drupal by investing in SEO-related initiatives that bring improvements and better technology to you.

6. Up-to-date—We make sure you're running the latest code on your Drupal website. Small updates can have a significant impact on your rankings.

7. Training—We have the best trained Drupal SEO specialists in the world.

8. The Drupal Way—We know how Drupal works. We follow the Drupal way which ensures your site is maintainable, updatable and secure.

9. Personal—You're more than just another website. You're part of the Drupal community. Yours is the site that Jenn designed and Bob built using the newest distribution from Jeff's company, and you're hosting with Eric. That's matters to us.

10. Results—With a ten-year track record of successful marketing engagements on Drupal websites, we can show you how to get to the top.

Marketing results faster, easier, and better with Drupal. That's Volacci - the Drupal SEO company.

Read more on the Volacci blog: *https://www.volacci.com/blog*